W9-DGP-638

New Relational Bible Studies
for Individuals and Groups

MEET ME
ON THE
PATIO

Karl A. Olsson

AUGSBURG PUBLISHING HOUSE
MINNEAPOLIS, MINNESOTA

MEET ME ON THE PATIO

MEET ME
ON THE
PATIO

Lowell Metzler

AUG 77

BGU

Contents

Preface

Favorable response to *Find Your Self in the Bible,* a modest introduction to relational Bible study, has encouraged me to publish a second volume of the same type of studies. This volume is intended not only to help readers develop relational life-styles, but to stimulate a relational use of the Bible throughout the church.

By "relational" I mean an emphasis on the personal, I-You, or bridging aspects of experience rather than the impersonal, external ones. For example, to know God "relationally" means to interact with him personally, face-to-face, to feel what he feels and to let him know what I am feeling. The same is true of my relationship with myself, significant others, and the world.

Such use of the Bible does not preclude scholarly biblical studies or theological and philosophical interpretation of the Scriptures. The art of tasty cooking does not render less valuable the sciences related to foods or to health. Both are needed.

Unfortunately, biblical and theological sciences have such prominence in our schools for preparing pastors that little time or energy is left to wrestle with how scriptural truth gets internalized, with how the bread of life gets eaten, masticated, and digested. Such internalizing (making the text one's own) comes less from communication of ideas, although that is certainly important, than from infusion of attitudes and feelings originating in the gospel, that is, from conveying a Christian life-style.

If I understand rightly the Scriptures and the history of the church, we are urged to allow the Holy Spirit to bring about the transformed life, that is, a life so open toward God, ourselves, and others that truth and love flow freely and creatively among us. I believe the Bible has been written to help us live such lives. As people of the Word, we are encouraged to read the Bible with this purpose in mind. It is my prayer that this book will help make the Bible more readable, more personal, and more relational.

Introductory notes

In the introductory chapters of *Find Your Self in the Bible,* I talked about my experience of making the Bible truly my book, God's living Word to me. I listed these four principles of relational Bible study which have proved helpful to me and to many others:

1. *Make the scriptural passage your own.* Put yourself into the story, not by transporting yourself into the ancient world and wearing a burnoose and sandals, but by identifying with the situation and message of the passage and seeing how they apply to your life and to lives of people close to you.

For instance, in Acts 9 we are told about the conversion of Saul of Tarsus. Saul was bent on stamping out the emerging Christian faith. He was on his way to Damascus with warrants for the arrest of any Christians he might find when he had a vision of the risen Lord and was called to account for his actions.

Meanwhile in Damascus the Lord called on a little known disciple, Ananias, to go to Saul and minister to him.

For us, the point of personal contact in the story is not the historical situation, important as that is, but rather the contemporary parallel it suggests. For example, where in our lives may we be using power to achieve conformity and stability? Or where, conversely, are we troubled by people and situations imposing control on us?

2. *Identify with a character and with his or her actions.* In Acts 9 we may identify with Saul as the controlling person or with Ananias as the person called by the Lord to minister to him.

Identification need not be limited to the nice people in the story or even to the not so nice. We may even, without sacrilege, get inside the mind of our Lord and identify with him in his relationships to the people around him.

3. *Find the gospel, or God's good news.* In the evangelical tradition, we do not turn to the Scriptures to find a moral principle or a spiritual discipline except insofar as they are vehicles of grace.

In the story of Saul, the gospel message is that, in spite of Saul's persecution of the church, the Lord stands ready to use him to witness to the Gentiles.

The gospel message for Ananias is that the work of grace may free the most unlikely people. We should note that, despite our misgivings, we can have a part in that work.

9

4. *Give the story (passage) a name.* The subject or title of the Bible study is more than a means of identifying it. It is a way to reach down into the deepest parts of yourself. It may make the truth of the passage speak not only to your intellect, but also to your memory, your imagination, your feelings, and your spirit, and in so doing bring about redemption within you.

Use of metaphor is an effective way of "reaching down" into one's psyche. Metaphor gives grace the vesture of an ordinary but highly significant experience in your life. Instances of the use of powerful "releasing" or "redemptive" metaphors might be G.K. Chesterton's "the inn does not lead to the road, the road leads to the inn, and all roads lead at last to the ultimate inn" and C.S. Lewis' description of Narnia as "the land where it's always winter and never Christmas."

Such use of metaphor is familiar from our life in the church. Baptism is a bath or a burial, Eucharist is a meal, the church is a body with limbs or a field in which seeds are planted.

By giving the Bible study a metaphoric name, grace or salvation can be powerfully conveyed. The dynamic of salvation in Saul's experience may be stated by the metaphor, "The Blinding that Gives Sight." Ananias' situation may be reflected by paraphrasing a best seller: "If You Meet Your Worst Enemy on the Road, Baptize Him."

These four principles do not constitute a science of relational Bible study. They are rough guidelines for getting into a text. They can be both challenged and modified as well as improved. But five years of experience by myself and others indicate that, through the Holy Spirit, these principles have helped the Bible come alive for many.

Group designs

This book is written for both individual and group use. Individuals may find the group designs at the end of each chapter helpful as a means of internalizing the Bible studies. I hope the designs will also be used by groups, since the process of studying the Bible together with other strugglers adds significant dimensions.

The following suggestions are offered for those who intend to use the book as a group study guide and resource.

1. The best results will probably follow if a study leader takes responsibility for discussing the chapter of the book being studied.

Having a different leader for each meeting is best. The pastor or the director of Christian education may need to serve as study leader initially, but the more people get involved, the better. Leaders need no professional theological training.

The leader may summarize salient points of the chapter and share personal experiences. He or she may want to respond to one or more of the questions being considered.

2. The leader should help the group break into smaller units. This may be done by forming new groups for each meeting or by initially forming groups of six or eight which break into twos, threes, or fours as suggested in the instructions for the chapter being studied.

3. The leader should be sensitive to how the group functions. The entire group may want to begin or close with singing and informal prayer. An opportunity for questions may be helpful. The small groups might be encouraged to close with intercessory prayer or corporate silence.

God has made me somebody

In the midst of the growing depersonalization of our time, it is comforting to hear voices encouraging us to be ourselves and stressing the value of personal identity. Being ourselves or doing "our own thing" helps break the spell of conformity and enables us to discover the joy of selfhood. Books such as *The One and Only You, Dare to Be You, Born to Win, I'm O.K., You're O.K.,* and a host of others sound this note.

Emphasis on humanity and selfhood is not new or merely humanistic. It is rooted deeply in scriptural truth. The personal identity theme may seem alien because we have become accustomed to thinking of Christians as selfless, unselfish, and self-denying. The call to accept and even delight in our selfhood seems worldly and scarily contrary to our Christian training.

And yet our faith stresses that God is our Creator, not only in a general sense as the watchmaker of the intricate chronometer of our universe, but specifically. He created the particular person which is you or me.

The first chapters of Genesis act as a zoom lens which moves from the farthest reaches of time and space into the burning center of our selfhood. The book begins in total formlessness and darkness. Everything is a vast nothing. But we are introduced immediately to God's brooding spirit—the intense, restless nature of the Creator. The words are simple but majestic: "In the beginning of Creation, when God made heaven and earth, the earth was without form and void, with darkness over the face of the abyss, and a mighty wind that swept over the surface of the waters. God said, 'Let there be light,' and there was light; and God saw that the light was good, and he separated light from darkness. He called the light day, and the darkness night. So evening came, and morning came, the first day" (Gen. 1-5 NEB).

From these words it is evident that God wanted to create. The divine desire is not motivated by caprice or ill will, in the manner of Thomas Hardy's cosmic "somnambulist," but by wisdom, love, and gladness. God wants to create what is good because he rejoices in what he makes.

The poetic image of the "morning stars singing together" expresses the fantastic gladness pervading the creative scene. God broods over the vastness and woos it toward harmony. All things move in free, purposive interrelatedness. It is like a stately dance in which all know their parts and their places, all accept them and rejoice in them. There is an urgent desire to call others into the dance, to "form" with them.

To create is to distinguish

The first words God speaks over the darkness are "Let there be light." The light is wisdom, logic. It brings order. It helps to distinguish and to differentiate. Light says, "This is this. It is not that." The water is not the land, plants are not animals, and animals are not human beings. All animals are not alike, and human beings are separated into individual persons.

To create is to give identity. The God who creates and orders also gives all things their special character. He draws a line around them and makes them unique.

Identity emerges. But things are not finished. Everything has the capacity to change and to grow. Everything is in the process of emerging. The light increases but is still peppered with darkness. The land emerges out of the sea, but the shoreline recedes again. In every grain of sand, in every living thing, something is unchanging and something is always in flux.

There is a mystery in our creation, for God chose to leave something unfinished and not yet created in us. God's creativity in us as well as our own creativity stems from our incompleteness. God intends something more in us and both he and we are involved in achieving it.

To decide to live and to grow is to accept the possibility of risk and pain, error and foolishness. Sometimes we will fail, and we will lose. But creativity takes place not in our perfection, but in our imperfection. That is why St. Augustine, while deploring the fall, argues that something more glorious than creation came from it, namely redemption.

God is at work expressing himself in the pain and joy of bringing something to being in us. He is not working without feeling. He feels the pain of our incompleteness. His creative work in us costs him something. We see the price in the cross.

We do not catch the heartbeat of the Scriptures if we

make God so unchangeably perfect and so without feeling that he does not touch us. The incarnation is an involvement which threatens the balance in the Godhead. It is a risk to the identity of God. Jesus became sin for us, says Paul, in order to make of us what God intended. How can we believe that God does not take risks in us to help us establish our final identity as persons?

Theologians have argued endlessly about Eden before the fall. Would it have been a place of change and decay, or of changelessness, or of change without decay? There are no answers to these questions. We do know that the tragedy of Eden was not change or even decay so much as falsehood and destructive confusion.

God accepts incompleteness but not deception, not disorder masked as an order which improves on God's design.

You will be like gods

This is the evil in the serpent's promise to Eve, "You will be like gods." God made human beings as creatures, not as creators. If you believe you are a god, you ignore your limitations, creatureliness, and mortality. Human beings do not have the power, wisdom, or goodness, the independence or permanence of God, no matter how frantically they try. Such confusion of self with God ends in destruction.

A second evil implied in the garden is presuming to be someone else. Eve presumes to act for Adam. Out of insecurity or uncertainty, out of arrogance and unhappiness about our identities, many of us presume to be someone else. We follow, we imitate, we over-identify with a pedestal person. We want to be that person. The effect is a stunting of our growth and a final sterility. When a woman gives up her last name in marriage, she may also give up her identity. That is a confusion of identities, or symbiosis.

Someone has illustrated it this way. The lines are symbols of people.

Relationship is like this.

Confusion or symbiosis is like this.

If two people confuse their identities, they lean on one another, give up their power to one another, and become one another in a sick way.

"A man leaves his father and mother and cleaves to his wife, *and they become one flesh.*" This powerful statement on marriage seems to advocate symbiosis, but it does not. Two "become one" in marriage, not to destroy the integrity of either person, but to find the intimacy of sexual union.

Camouflaging our humanity

There is a final temptation—becoming not a god or another person but something subhuman, a snake or a worm. After disobedience Adam and Eve look for camouflage, not only to hide their nakedness, but also to hide from God. Instead of appearing before God in the glory of their original humanity, they hide furtively "among the trees of the garden," like the serpent who seduced them. They need to make themselves as insignificant as possible so they won't feel the pain of being human and hence responsible.

17

There is something comforting, relaxing about not being a man or a woman. An insect can disappear under the molding. But to be human means that you do not try to be God on the one hand, or try to creep into subhuman identities on the other. I once knew a clergyman who often talked about being a worm. "I am a worm," he would say, "and no man." He apologized for his existence. He wriggled his way through life.

In the piece on the Grand Inquisitor in *The Brothers Karamazov,* Dostoevsky tells us that the church has tried to make people into chickens. The message is, "Be little chickens. Stay in the coop, we'll take care of you. We'll feed you and give you water and protect you. We'll even let you sin a little bit. But be chickens. Peacefully you will live and peacefully you will die."

D.H. Lawrence says that people have become doggy, tail-wagging, anxious to please, licking up crumbs from the master's table. He suggests that men should be proud and wear red pants. That's happened, of course. We wear bright-colored pants today. I wonder though if sometimes we do not continue our tail-wagging even in our flowered pants. We would like to be just Airedales, beloved by everybody, patted on the head and thrown a bone now and then, allowed to live in the corner, unchallenged to be who we really are.

Daphne du Maurier tells a story of a vicious clergyman who plots all kinds of evil. In the drawer of his desk is found a picture of his congregation. They are all sheep and little lambs. Baaa-aa. They sit stupidly, docilely, sheepishly. They are sheep not in the sense of being God's flock, but in the sense of being silly. And when you get a sheepy notion of yourself and go through life wagging

18

your stumpy little tail and baaa-ing at everybody, or when you act as a worm, a chicken, or a dog, you are not living up to your identity as a person.

We are human, we are persons—every one of us. That means we can emerge. As the land rose out of the sea, so we can emerge at God's call and become everything he has intended us to be. We are going to be in process all our lives, working on our identities. God has in effect said to us in Christ, "Sometimes you have committed the sin of arrogance, but more often you have committed the sin of needless submission and subservience, as if you were ashamed to be the person I created you to be."

The second creation

The Bible tells us about the first creation, which has launched us, together with amoebas and galaxies, into a stream of change, growth, and fulfillment.

But one of the glories of that first creation—and God's greatest risk—human freedom, went sour. Instead of choosing light and truth, our primal parents and we in them chose darkness and deception. From that choice has come a strange and sinister twisting of human history. The tragedy of that history is that it cannot by its own efforts become untwisted again.

But God did not give up on his creation. The Bible tells us an incredible story, namely, that God himself became human to restore our identities and to reestablish relationships with us. In Jesus God entered human history, identified himself with us, and brought us healing.

His message was the great value of all created things, even of flowers and sparrows, but particularly of people.

People are so precious that in Jesus God gave himself as a ransom to buy them back from the forces of deception and destruction. The moving message of the New Testament is that people—individual persons—are the object of God's mercy and that all can become new creatures through that mercy.

To be new creatures means not claiming a different identity but rather seeing one's original self cleansed, healed, and restored. Because of God's love for me I can understand who I am, I can accept and even delight in myself.

The Christ who heals us is also the guardian of our identity, the shepherd of our souls. The New English Bible translates part of Psalm 23, "He renews life within me, and for his name's sake guides me in the right path."

In C.S. Lewis' *The Lion, the Witch, and the Wardrobe,* we are introduced to Aslan, the lion. He is a gigantic, golden-maned animal, ferocious and gentle, "good and terrible at the same time." Aslan offers up his life as a ransom to free young Edmund from the grasp of the White Witch. Aslan is then raised from death and does battle against the Witch and all the enemies of the created world.

Aslan is a Christ figure in which the Lord's power over evil is dramatically conveyed. This figure says to me that Christ is more than capable of dealing with all the enemies of my identity because in the cross he has vanquished them one and all: the forces of deception, confusion, camouflage, self-loathing, and self-destruction. Within the circle of his strength and mercy I can delight in who I am.

To have Christ as guardian of my soul, however, does

not allow me to remain where I am. "He renews my life." In the words of another well-known psalm, he forgives my sin and heals all my diseases. When I am in Christ's presence I am in the process of being healed. And this goes on until the very end of my life.

I have a 92-year-old mother. She says to me, "Why do preachers think that because I am old, I can't be responsible or keep on growing? They preach sermons about heaven and that's OK, but they don't deal with us as people who can still fail and sin and who need forgiveness and absolution."

Often when I call my mother we talk about relationships, the meaning of grace, the power of prayer in her life and in the lives of those she loves. That is very exciting to me. Even though she is old, she remains a person. She is not just a role: a golden ager, a retiree, a senior citizen. She keeps her identity. That's what Christ wants us to be: persons, not chickens or sheep. He wants us to be persons whom God has created and who keep on being redeemed.

One summer I had a very enlightening experience at a training event for leaders. I was in a group of five people. At the end of the week we had a feedback session, inviting comments from others on how we had performed as leaders. We made a chair in the circle into the hot seat and we took turns sitting in it. Then we asked the others to tell us honestly what they thought our strong points were and particularly what areas we needed to work on.

It was a very healthy but not entirely painless experience. With one voice and with one accord my group said to me, "The negative feeling we have about your leadership this week is that you have been so afraid to lead that you have consistently denied your gifts. You have power but you are sitting on it. That makes us mad because you are depriving us of your gifts. Are you trying to be nice?"

I said to myself, "Of course. I want to be approved and liked and seen not as a driving, directive person but as an affirming, gentle soul. I want to be an inoffensive, washed-out beige."

I confessed to the group, "I sometimes feel as if I'm driving a 20-ton truck that can go 120 miles per hour, and I am driving that rig at 15 miles per hour because I don't want to discourage pedestrians or the tractor that is moving in a parallel field at two miles an hour."

The group asked me, "Don't you see that as an insult to the pedestrian and the tractor?" And, of course, it is.

I came out of that experience with the feeling that I had failed. I had failed to accept the gift of myself. I had betrayed myself and the group, but I had also betrayed the process and even Christ himself.

The group said to me, "Let your truck run at full speed. Don't sit on your power. If the truck runs too fast for us and threatens to run over us, we'll let you know. Trust us. And let us worry about ourselves. Don't try to protect us."

Then I thought about how often I had tried to protect people from myself and others. I victimized them and didn't allow them to grow up. Small children may need protection, though not nearly so much as we imagine, but adults need the space and freedom to make mistakes, to get hurt, to grow, to learn, to become.

I have spoken of Jesus as the guardian of our souls. This may suggest that Jesus is in the business of protecting us from life and from one another. But that's not the case at all. What Jesus guards is our inalienable right to be ourselves. He keeps us honest and enables us to face into the wind. He helps us to battle the things in us which are devious and deceptive and which thus tend to destroy personhood.

Jesus' purpose in living, dying, and being raised, his purpose in coming to us, is to keep us from falling and to bring us faultless and joyous before his glorious presence. Christ's work is to see restored in us God's original intent, but now so immeasurably deepened and enriched by the work of grace that we are a new creation in him.

GROUP DESIGN 1

After presentation of the Bible study on Genesis 1:1-4, "God Has Made Me Somebody," with personal modeling and sharing by the leader, the total group should form into fours or sixes, remaining in the same room.

This design is in two parts, a guided fantasy and related questions.

Ask participants to make themselves comfortable, to close their eyes, and to focus on the creation scene as it is developed. A suggested fantasy follows, but the leader may want to develop his or her own.

Guided fantasy

Let's imagine that we have been transported to the very beginning of creation as it is recorded in the Bible. All we can see and experience on every side is primal darkness unbroken by starlight or moonlight or any sign of life. No fires are burning, no candles are lit. Everything is vast, black, and undifferentiated.

Then in the middle of the blackness is the beginning of motion. At first it is only a breath. Then it begins to grow until the vastness of abyss—like endless ocean waters without color, taste, or sound—is shaken as by a great wind.

And in the midst of the darkness and the restless motion, God says, "Let there be light!" That is the moment of creation. Now we can see the darkness rushing back into the infinities, back and back as clouds flee away, and light and order emerge. God creates. He separates and distinguishes. He draws a line between the great waters. He allows the land to emerge out of the sea.

At first the sea is steaming hot and then pleasantly warm. Here and there across the surface in creative playfulness, we see the land appear—mountains, islands, and continents.

At first the land is too hot for things to grow, but now slowly it is covered with fine green vegetation and then by tropical forests. And we see the great animals of the past, both in the sea and on the land, and above us in the air there are myriads of birds.

In the midst of that creation is a garden called Eden where God brings into existence a special creation—upright, noble, and beautiful beings made in his image. To them he gives the power of intellect and will and dominion over the world he has created. We are not separate from these first people. We are they. We are the man and the woman. We feel the creative touch of the God who made us.

Now let us see ourselves personally in the midst of Eden, involved with our own creation. It is a fantastic morning: flowers bursting into bloom, birds trying new songs, animals tumbling on velvet lawns. And God's strong, gentle hands are on you and me, fashioning us into beings in his image. We can feel his breath on us like a wind blowing in from the sea. That breath enters us and gives us life and something of his spirit.

As God touches you and me, let us think of the things which make us uniquely who we are. What is our essence, our particular character, our flavor?

Questions

To give questions focus, invite participants to identify with one or more of the following characteristics in response to the question, How do I see myself? The list may be read while people remain with their eyes closed. Give ample time between each statement.

I SEE MYSELF AS:

1. Leading. Having charisma, a quality which makes it easy for people to follow me.

2. Supportive. Not initiating but caring for and maintaining.

3. Solitary. Rather by myself than interacting with others.

4. Ordering and controlling. Needing to give things structure and rules.

5. Feeling. Asking, How do people feel? rather than, How do they function?

6. Sensitive and artistic. More aware of the sense stimuli of things (color, sound, feel, touch, taste, composition, design) than their practical value.

7. Analyzing. Taking things apart to understand and perhaps control them.

8. Observing. Standing and looking rather than jumping in and participating.

9. Comical. Tending to see the lighter side.

10. Verbal. Needing to put things into words to assimilate them.

11. Active. Restless when nothing is being done.

12. Meditative. Thinking about things deeply and needing quiet.

13. Prayerful and devotional.

14. Sociable. Enjoying other people.

15. Impulsive. Daring. Taking risks without much calculation.

16. Deliberate. Needing time to think before acting.

Then ask participants to share within their small groups the descriptive statements with which they identify. Additional questions for this design are:

1. How do I feel about accepting this *me* as part of God's design?

2. What would I like to do or what have I done to complete my identity?

Claiming
my power

A word of Jesus is recorded in John 10:18: "No one takes my life away from me. I give it up of my own free will. I have the right to give it, and I have the right to take it back."

The more we know about who we are, the more we can accept that, and the more wholeness we have, the more certainly God's spirit can move through us and the more power we have.

We are not talking about power as control. Control is external power a person assumes out of insecurity. Hence control need not be real power. Real power comes from God. When there is an equation between who I am and the power I exercise, then I am in balance and I can be a creative person and feel OK about myself. To not feel OK about myself may cause me to try to control situations which are beyond my power.

Samson losing his power

The story of Samson in Judges 13–16 is often made fun of and perhaps never quite fully understood. Heaven took a special interest in Samson. His coming was announced by an angel. He was given to his parents and to his nation for a purpose. When he became a young man the Spirit was given to him, and that Spirit or that power actually *was* Samson. As long as he retained his identity and his sense of living and acting by that God-given power, he accomplished the things he set out to do.

Samson had two gifts, one of which is sometimes ignored. He had wit and he had strength. But in two instances he gave up his intellectual power to the Philistines and as a result lost all power.

Samson was given to Israel to deal with the problem of the Philistines. Yet the first thing he did when he became an adult was to marry a Philistine, a woman of Timnah. As Samson was going to Timnah, the spirit of the Lord came upon him, and he tore a lion limb from limb. Later when he passed the place of the killing, bees had created a honeycomb inside the lion's carcass. Samson and his parents ate the honey. He formulated a riddle out of that, promising gifts to the wedding guest who could solve it: "Out of the eater came something to eat. Out of the strong came something sweet." His Philistine wife coaxed and manipulated him until, contrary to his best judgment, he gave her the answer to the riddle. She told the Philistines, which began the undoing of Samson. The Philistines burned up Samson's wife.

This episode set up probability for the next one.

Samson fell in love with a second Philistine, Delilah. Delilah probed him for the secret of his strength. Samson told her, "If you bind me with seven green bowstrings, I will lose my strength." She bound him and the Philistines tried to overpower him, but Samson broke the strings and disposed of them easily.

Then Delilah said, "Come on now, Samson, you're not

telling me the truth. What is the secret of your strength?" And he said, "If you will bind me with new ropes, you will have me." So she bound him with new ropes and the Philistines came. But again Samson broke their ropes.

Then Delilah got even angrier. She said, "You must tell me your secret." And he said, "Well, weave my locks in with the web in the loom and I will become weak." She did that and he tore his hair out of the loom.

Then Delilah applied the final pressure. She nagged him day after day until his soul was "vexed to death." Finally he told her, "If you really want the secret of my strength, cut my hair. I will lose my strength because I am a Nazirite and I have dedicated my life to the Lord. My strength is in my dedicated hair." When she had learned his secret, she called in the Philistine lords. They shaved his head, put his eyes out, and made him a slave, and he ground corn in the prison house at Gaza. But when his hair grew out again, he tore down the house of Dagon. Three thousand Philistines were killed.

The heart of the story is this: Samson was manipulated to yield his power to someone else without God's permission. Samson was not like Jesus, who said, "I give up my life, and I have the right to take it back." Jesus gave up his life but not his identity, his power. But Samson handed over his power. The Middle Ages used to call that "selling your soul to the Devil."

A bad bargain

I submit that this is how we most often lose our effectiveness and our creativity. We trade away our power, our identity, our being, for something less. It happens all the time. In Christian history during the great persecutions, there were people who were called traitors. When the pressure was on them and they were asked, "Are you a Christian? Is this your identity?" they said, "No, we are not Christians. We abjure the name of Christ." They were scared and they capitulated. The time they bought was tainted.

We have seen the same thing among subjugated people who give up their power much too quickly. We have seen it in submissive women and in submissive men. They have given over their power to someone who had no right to it. The result has been destruction of identity and destruction of creativity.

We do that today. I have done it, I have seen it done, and I have brought it about in people. It happens all the time, and it is very destructive, both for us personally and for the people we associate with. To give someone your power is not to help but ultimately to destroy him or her.

For instance, we may give someone the power to dominate us and to manipulate us. And when we do that, we have given up the best part of ourselves. People who become overly dependent on us may also have our power. They can "hook" us and call the shots. Because we "need to be needed" and like to have people dependent on us, we may transfer our power to them. Then we are under their command.

We give someone the power to use us in this way when we're afraid to say no. It happens in the church. We give up our right to self-determination and we become snowed under by responsibilities we don't want to carry because we don't dare to say, "I can't do that" or "I don't want to do it" or "I'm not going to do it." In the church we have thousands and thousands of lay people who have handed over their power to the religious professionals. It sometimes looks as if the church exists for the sake of the clergy. That is being changed now, but through past surrenders many lay people with power and identity and creativity have given it all up. They have done what Samson did, giving away the secret of their strength.

Parents sometimes do this with children. They have given the children their power, opening the door to bribery and permissiveness. Because no one is willing to stand up and be his or her own person, children and parents both suffer.

Why the bad bargain?

Why did Samson give up his power? Why do we give up ours? Why would you give up your identity, the most precious thing you have, to someone else?

Perhaps the chief reason is to avoid conflict. Samson can pick up the jawbone of an ass and kill off a thousand Philistines. He seems to have all kinds of courage. But with two women, he is like putty. He can only deal with physical conflict. He cannot put his spirit over against the spirit of these persuasive women. He loses his head, his wit, his judgment.

Sometimes we give up our power because we think that to be good Christians and to show love means to comply, to please, to be nice. We have been carefully taught to be nice. The most important thing in life, we have been told, is to be pleasant and to avoid conflict.

Husbands and wives are nice to one ~~another~~ not honest, but nice. And they give up their power.

Sometimes I give up my power because I don't want to pay the price to keep it. I may give it up to avoid the responsibility of being an adult. To be adult is free and exciting, but it is also very difficult. And so, instead of paying the price of being an adult, rather than take risks and bear the pain of being accountable, I give up my adulthood and let someone else become an adult for me.

In the process of abdicating our power, we waste a great deal of energy. It's as if we use all the energy we can command to keep ourselves in a position of powerlessness. We lose a sense of wholeness; we lost our creativity.

Against that background of draining away creativity, draining away identity, draining away power, I want to tell you a little of my own story. I have learned a great deal about myself, and I'd like to share what I've learned with you.

Some time ago I was acting in ways that robbed me of energy without my knowing it. I began to feel very tired. I was always dreaming about going to bed. The constant image before my eyes was not a gourmet meal or an ordinary enticing scene, but just a nice bed. I got up in the morning and I wanted to go to bed. And I wanted to go to bed for only one reason, which was to rest, to sleep, or maybe to die. It got to the point where I was so tired that I began thinking of early retirement. Retirement had the double enticement of going to bed and getting out of my job.

I also got sick. I had a series of respiratory infections. One started in the summer and really knocked me out and then it stayed with me for several months. The following February I got so sick I had to go to bed for a month with the old infection, or a new one. When I got up, the doctor found that I had hypertension and ordered a dreary succession of tests and medications.

Effects of losing power

In the midst of all this, I began to lose my creativity. I began to lose my sense of identity. I began to lose my initiative. I began to lose my interest in putting things together. My life, my work, and the things I usually enjoy doing felt flat and stale. I became apathetic. People would say to me, "Are you taking some kind of sedation? You look as if you are on Librium or Valium." I was taking drugs to bring my blood pressure down, but that wasn't my problem. My apathy was deeper than that induced by the medication.

I didn't know what was the matter until I discovered to my amazement that for about two and a half years I had been progressively giving away my power. I was functioning within narrower and narrower limits. I never expressed an honest opinion for fear that I would hurt someone. I never acted decisively for fear that I would rock the boat. After I'd recovered, I mentioned this to a friend, a very perceptive person, and she said, "I noticed that. I noticed that you were much nicer than you normally are. I thought it was sort of sick." And I said, "It was." It is.

Without knowing it, and imperceptibly, I had been transfering my power over to other people because I didn't want to be responsible for decisions. I became nicer and nicer, in fact so nice that I was stupid. I had my thumb in my mouth. I was feeling sorry for myself. My attitude was passive. I felt like Samson with all his hair gone.

I decided all this had gone far enough, and I was going to turn the whole busines around and begin to act decisively. And I did. I did something extremely painful for me and extremely painful for some other people. But I made a decision and I communicated the decision. And I suddenly discovered a polarization of support around me which I hadn't known existed. My friends had been standing with their thumbs in their mouths too, not knowing what to do about me and not being able to act about me because I didn't give them an opportunity.

Reclaiming power

At a training event, we were asked to come up with a dream or a hope for the future. Suddenly I saw that to have an identity and to be my own person meant that I did not have the right to give myself away. I did not have the right to let myself erode. I did not have the right to stop dreaming. I did not have the right to doubt in the miraculous power of God. I had the same feeling Samson had in the prison house. My strength returned to me, my hair grew out.

When the Lord came to Sarah and Abraham and said, "You are going to have a son," Sarah laughed. I too had been laughing at instead of accepting the miracle. Realizing that, I began to think of some bold things for the future.

I was about to leave my job. I had been thinking of that as a step toward erosion. Now I decided that I was going to say what Ulysses says in Tennyson's poem, "We are not now that strength which in old days moved earth and heaven, but what we are, we are." And suddenly I began to feel at home with my identity and I began to feel at home with my power, and I decided that I was still going to do some effective things with my life.

For many years I have been reading Shakespeare's *King Lear* with deep appreciation, but I never got hold of the tragedy of Lear until recently. As King Lear begins to grow old, he decides to split up his kingdom among his three daughters: Goneril, Regan, and Cordelia. He does this, he says, so he may give over his responsibilities and "unburdened, crawl toward death." In the distribution ceremony, Goneril and Regan flatter the old king and make promises to him which they do not intend to keep. Only Cordelia is straight with him and refuses to say the sweet things he expects to hear. As a result he disinherits her. As soon as Lear has given up the power to Goneril and Regan, they proceed to violate their agreements with him, and he is left at last with nothing.

Shakespeare was a monarchist. He believed that kingship brought about a fusion of a man's personal identity and his identity as king. That meant that a king had no right to do what Lear did, even though he was old and tired. To give up his royal power was to relinquish his personal power. The pathos of Lear is that, once his crown is gone, he begins to dissolve as a person. He becomes querulous, impotent, and railing. What majesty is left resembles a dying echo.

Although I am not a king, I have no right to relinquish use of the gifts God has given me until he frees me to do so. Simeon puts it well: "You may let your servant go in peace." When permission is given, but only then, can we go.

The story of Samson really began to speak to me. I have no intention of tearing down the temple of Dagon and killing 3000 Philistines, but I want to claim the power the Holy Spirit gives me and to use that power as long as I can. I have no business sitting down in a chair with a thermometer in my mouth and a mug of warm milk, tc wait for death.

I want to call you to claim your power and your identity. I want to call you to the great creative adventure of being yourself. I want you to believe that you are someone, that God made you into someone, and that you have power. If you have given away your power, reclaim it, and enjoy your identity. Luxuriate in it, and celebrate it. You should love your neighbor as yourself. That means to love yourself, celebrate yourself, and delight in yourself.

It's beautiful to see Jesus in this light. Jesus has been pictured as meek and mild, but he was indestructible. When he went up to meet the devil in the wilderness right after his baptism, the devil tried to take his power away from him in three temptations, and Jesus said to him, in effect, "Take your temptations back to hell with you! That's where they belong and where you belong." And an angel came and comforted him.

That will happen to you too. Just tell the devil to go to hell, and that you'll keep your power. That's what Jesus meant when he told Pilate, "You can't control me because I've got my power. I've got me and God has me—you don't."

One of my favorite passages is by Meister Eckart: "God delights in himself like a young horse galloping across a green and level plain. Because that's a horse's nature." God delights in himself and we delight in ourselves, not because we aren't filled with sin and weakness. We are. But we are also wonderful, because God has made us that way. And that's what we want to celebrate.

GROUP DESIGN 2

This design may require a smaller group and a higher level of confidentiality. Groups of two or three are suggested, preferably with people not too well known to one another. It may be helpful to review briefly what we mean by "giving someone else our power." (It is the action whereby we stop being ourselves and over-identify with someone else.) A related topic is why we relinquish power, and still another, the effects of doing that. We also want to give the process a positive turn by indicating possible steps toward the recovery of power.

When groups are formed and everyone understands the topic, the following questions may be presented. (It is advisable to put them on newsprint or a blackboard so they may be readily referred to.)

1. Where in my life am I tempted to give away my power? Why?

2. What effect has this behavior had on me?

3. What am I willing and able to do to reclaim that power?

Because of the close interrelation of the questions, each person in the small group may discuss all three questions without interruption. A 10 to 15 minute time slice for each participant is suggested.

Life on
the patio

We've been dealing in the first two chapters with the meaning of our identity. In Chapter 2, we dealt with the question of how management of identity affects freedom. I would now like to take that a step further. While we need to "do our own thing," we must remember that we are not islands. We cannot have identities and power unless we live in relationship.

Relationship or community is a mystery from the very beginning, even in the reality of the Trinity. "It is not good that man should be alone," but neither, seemingly, is it good for God. From the beginning, there has been community in the Trinity— Father, Son, and Holy Spirit.

But what does it mean for us human beings to live in relationship? Human nature being gregarious, all sorts of associations and communities have emerged to meet human needs. People are jammed together in families, tribes, nations, clubs, congregations, and cliques.

Sometimes we get confused in using the term *relationship*. We equate it with other forms of togetherness. In his epistle to the Corinthians, Paul talks about God's design for relationship as expressed in Christ's body, the family of grace:

> Christ is like a single body, which has many parts; it is still one body, even though it is made up of different parts. In the same way, all of us, Jews and Gentiles, slaves and free men, have been baptized into the one body by the same Spirit, and we have all been given the one Spirit to drink (1 Cor. 12:12-13).

When we talk about claiming our power or celebrating our identity, we are not speaking of an indifference to other members of the community. We are all interrelated in the bundle of life. How we deal with our power is important not only to us but also to other members of the community.

The way to give up our power utterly is to dissociate ourselves from a community. It's no solution to say, "Well, I'm going to do my thing. I'm going to be alone and independent and sever all my relationships because I can't stand to get into the risk and pain of being with people." When you dissociate yourself (except for a reason, as Paul says about marriage), when you absent yourself permanently from the human race, you end up without an authentic selfhood and without power.

The twin towers

How does it look to be related to other people? On page 42 is a simple drawing of two towers representing me and you. The towers stand on a common foundation, sharing the sub-floor. Down in the foundation, the basement area, you and I are bound together by our common humanity. Whether we like it or not, we all have shared needs. Abraham Maslow talks about common human needs stretching from basic needs for food, drink, and shelter, through needs for security, love, belonging, and self-esteem, to the need for self-actualization. Everybody has these needs. Our color and our social status don't matter on this level, because we are bound together in the bundle of human needs.

We also are bound together by a community of feelings. We all feel the same things. In his argument with Christians in *The Merchant of Venice,* Shylock says:

> Hath not a Jew eyes? Hath not a Jew hands, organs, dimensions, senses, affections, passions?—fed with the same food, hurt with the same weapons, subject to same diseases, healed by the same means, warmed and cooled by the same winter and summer as a Christian is? If you prick us, do we not bleed?

Our feelings of anger, fear, anxiety, grief, hate, love, joy, and hope are common human feelings. In this respect, there is no difference between me and an aborigine of Australia. We both feel. We are also bound together because we all have a history. Everybody has lived in time. Everyone passes through a sequence of events from birth to death. We are all together in the basement.

But as soon as we move up above this basement floor, there is differentiation. The first floor, which we shall call the patio, is *personhood*. God has made each of us a unique individual. Though we still share basic human needs, at this level we are different. We each have a separate, God-given identity. On the patio—the level of personhood—we struggle equally with our healing and wholeness. And this is where we meet, where we can communicate directly.

The next floor we call *talent*. Here for the first time we

TWIN TOWERS

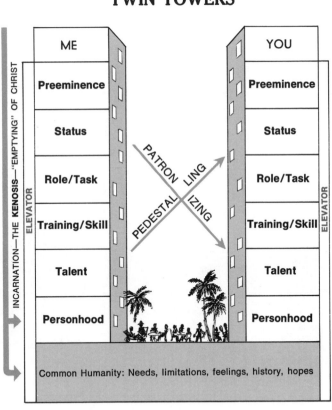

can begin to quantify and measure. One person's talent is obviously greater in some ways than another person's talent. You sing better than I do. I may draw better than you do. Talent is what we are born with. That's given in us and it comes in through the DNA and all the other biochemical factors which determine us. It's part of our computer. If you go back 5000 years, the printed circuits which will combine in you are present in your ancestors. And that means that you may have more measurable talent than I do or I may have more than you, which could make us competitive.

The next floor level in the tower we call *skills and training*. I take the talent I have and I give it training. And that means that we face another differentiation, because although I may be talented, my talent needs to be shaped. I can be Tarzan of the Apes and have a fantastic baritone voice with which to yell as I swing from limb to limb, but unless I train that voice and make it a usable skill, I will not go very far.

The next level, closely related to training and skills, is what we call *roles or tasks*. These are functions we assume or which are laid on us by the community. We carry the roles of parents and children, husbands and wives, teachers and students, doctors and patients, pastors and lay persons, merchants and customers.

A traditional society with a slow rate of change tends to place nearly all identity in roles. This is true of the military establishment, where, with few exceptions, rank is role. The behavior of a soldier is largely determined by his role. Swedish telephone books are still careful about giving role identifications in listing numbers. Even authors are listed by that designation. In the past, such role distinctions have been carried over to the wives of professional people. In some European cultures, it is important in address to give the proper feminine variant for the wife of a provost or bishop.

A host of privileges, expectations, traditions, and rules of etiquette are associated with nearly every role. Until recently, the role of women provided some immunities and rights. Women could usually expect seats on the bus, their chairs pulled out for them, and the car door opened. They were also protected from certain kinds of humor and left out of conversations concerning matters of intellectual complexity.

The next level of the tower is *status*. This is a floor which the community designates as special. It is reserved for those who, in the exercise of their skills or tasks or roles, have been able to lift their heads a little above the crowd. This is the floor of Who's Who, the Social Register, and the honors which oil the civic machinery.

The final level is *preeminence*. This is the penthouse of the tower. It is elegant with gold leaf ceilings, crystal chandeliers, deep pile carpeting, fabulous furniture. Here all sound is muted, all discord banned, all mess eliminated. Everything is discreet, courteous, calm, and slightly chilled.

On the floor of preeminence, I am vastly lonely and almost entirely public. I open the door to go out and I am besieged by reporters, news and television cameras, and gossip columnists. My medical reports are studied and my opinions probed; my family is grilled, my past X-rayed, my religious life screened. I cannot have an un-challenged taste, feeling, need, or urge.

The telephone rings with a muted musical sound, but it rings incessantly. The rooms are huge, but a line of

44

people is always waiting outside. In the penthouse, the trivial is often magnified and the significant is trivialized, and yet the urge is not down to commonness but upward toward super-eminence.

Connections

How does the "me" tower relate to the "you" tower? People of similar talents develop relationships, especially when talent develops into skill. For example, star athletes gravitate to one another. They have a straight, level bridging which is more associational than relational, that is, the connections between them depend more on what they do than on what they are as persons. The same holds true for musicians, artists, professors, poets, and others. Many of our relationships or associations are determined by skill. role, or task.

For many of us, associational patterns may be entirely determined by role. I may be a doctor who is always a doctor. I treat my family as if they were patients, especially patients who have been waiting too long in the waiting room. Or, probably more common, I may be a preacher who thinks of his family as a congregation.

Part of this is inevitable. There have to be parents and children. There have to be husbands and wives. There have to be pastors and parishioners, doctors and patients, lawyers and clients. Roles help to expedite our lives. If you drive into the gas station to get gas, and you ask the attendant to fill up the tank, he does not expect you to go into his inner life, nor do you expect him to ask about your family relationships, since all you want is to have the tank filled. It would be very tedious if you got into a line to buy an airplane ticket and the man at the desk and the passenger in front of you were involved in a 45-minute conversation on how to handle their feelings.

But our society is made up almost entirely of such formal associations. People on balconies are waving and shouting at one another and never touching one another. People in Congress or a courtroom or a professional meeting have a hallooing full of traditional courtesy and even pleasantry but often falling short of relationship. The pattern of association is formal and hierarchical, so little genuine interaction takes place.

Let me summarize briefly. In the two towers, the "me" tower and the "you" tower, we have the following possibilities for meeting:

• We can make contact at the talent, training, skill, role, status, and preeminence levels by acknowledging people at the same levels in the other towers in what might be called a nodding or hallooing acquaintance. Competitiveness and envy are probable.

• We can also make contact by two nonlevel motions:

1) Patronizing, that is, looking down on people below us in talent, skill, training, or status; or

2) pedestaling, that is, looking up to idealize or idolize people above us in the tower.

• We can meet on the patio in our personhoods.

The towers of Philippi

The Bible provides insights into our consideration of the towers. It describes our life together on the patio in Philippians 2:1-11:

46

Does your life in Christ make you strong? Does his love comfort you? Do you have fellowship with the Spirit? Do you feel kindness and compassion for one another? I urge you, then, make me completely happy by having the same thoughts, sharing the same love, and being one in soul and mind. Don't do anything from selfish ambition, or from a cheap desire to boast; but be humble toward each other, never thinking you are better than others. And look out for each other's interests, not just for your own. The attitude you should have is the one that Christ Jesus had: He always had the very nature of God, but he did not think that by force he should try to become equal with God. Instead, of his own free will he gave it all up, and took the nature of a servant. He became like man, and appeared in human likeness. He was humble and walked the path of obedience to death —his death on the cross. For this reason God raised him to the highest place above, and gave him the name that is greater than any name. At the name of Jesus, all beings in heaven, on earth, and in the world below will fall on their knees, and all will openly proclaim that Jesus Christ is the Lord, to the glory of God the Father.

If I understand the situation among believers in the church at Philippi, the first tide of freedom and joy and love and harmony, which had been theirs in their exposure to the gospel, had receded. Although little tidal pools of inspiration remained, they were no longer carried and nourished by their first love.

In Chapter 2 of the letter, the apostle pointedly discusses the Philippians' love and compassion for one another, and in Chapter 4 he becomes even more specific about Euodia and Syntyche, two women witnesses in the church who have worked effectively for the gospel but who are now at odds.

What emerges in these passages is a fairly common phenomenon among primitive Christians: the desire for status and envy of those who achieve it. Among Jesus' disciples we see this in the aspirations of James and John to be seated at Jesus' right and left hand in his kingdom. It is also present in the wrangling in the Upper Room. Paul finds it in churches other than Philippi, notably Rome and Corinth. When Clement of Rome wrote his epistle to the Corinthians toward the close of the first century, he bewailed the envy and sedition in the ranks of Corinthian Christians.

Christians who once started on the patio together have begun to climb up into the tower. They are claiming the talent, skill, role, or status which puts them above fellow believers. They are cashing in on their work for Christ by claiming that it gives them a higher place in the tower.

In a brief autobiographical passage in Philippians 3:4-6, Paul tells about his right to a place high in his own tower. He talks about his circumcision, his status as an Israelite of the tribe of Benjamin; he reminds them that he is a pureblooded Hebrew and no proselyte. He has been associated with the Pharisees and his zeal once led him to persecute the church. His obedience of the Law has been flawless.

I understand the situation in Philippi because that is the situation in my world and in my fellowship. When we feel insecure and scared, we scurry up in our towers and find some temporary safety in being above and controlling people rather than identifying with them.

And I identify with Paul, because for much of my life, despite protestations of modesty and humility, I have been trying to clamber up in the tower toward status and even preeminence. I have had the advantage of being born a male WASP, of pure Aryan stock and Nordic kin. I completed the training to make me a priest in the church of my birth; my zeal for that church gave me status and eminence if not preeminence. Within the church I followed the educational route; within the community I became a respected leader in those benevolent enterprises where I may have been charged with ambition but never with greed.

When I began writing books, I yearned for the preeminence of the writer of a best seller. I read my reviews anxiously and looked with envious eyes on those who wrote better books than I or who wrote books on the same topic which sold better.

So far, I have couched this in the past tense, but let me be candid. I can also write it in the present. I still spend too much time up in the tower worrying about my competitors in relational theology—the leaders, speakers, writers, teachers, trainers—and I'm still fearful lest their reputation eclipse mine.

Christ on the patio

But there is gospel. In the midst of the wrangling at Philippi, Paul helps the ambitious, envious Christians, frenziedly climbing their towers, to remember whose people they are. He reminds them of Jesus, who could have snatched at the preeminence of the Father but who took an opposite course. Instead of claiming the top of the tower, he came down to us. He united with us in our humanity and personhood; he became like us and joined us on the patio. He was Emmanuel—"God with us." Here he lived and suffered and died, not because he was a man claiming to be God, but because he was God, wanting to be one of us.

Paul says, "He became like man, and appeared in human likeness. He was humble and walked the path of obedience to death—his death on the cross" (Phil. 2:7b-8). And because he came down and built the elevator shaft and installed and empowered the elevator, those of us who are up in the tower and would like to get down to the patio are enabled to do so.

We sometimes fancy that if we could go up in the tower to the very top and mingle with the "beautiful people," the powerful, the wealthy, and the elite, we would be closer to him. But the higher we get in the tower and the more infrequently we visit the patio, the lonelier we get and the further we get away from him.

This doesn't mean that all the world's powerful stay away from the patio and are only penthouse people. We need only think of truly great souls like Abraham, President Lincoln, Pope John XXIII, and many others to remember that there are preeminent people who find their home on the patio.

I hear Pope John saying to the world from the top of the ecclesiastical tower, "I'm lonely up here. I serve here because I am called to be here, but I don't want to *live* here. This isn't my home. I want to be where people are. I came from lowly people and I want to go down to the patio where Jesus is. I want to be a person to persons."

The gospel is that Jesus has opened the way for us to God through the patio.

The pedestal

I am an insecure, anxious person. When I flee into my talents or my training or my skill or depend on my role and what status I have, I do so because I am scared.

During the years when I lived more as a public figure than as a private person, I am sure I found some ego satisfactions in being Number One. For a while it was a blast to be invited to the chief place at the feast and always to sit at the speaker's table. But my deepest motivation was not ego esteem so much as fear. If I could occupy a place in the tower, you could not so easily get at me and see my teeth chattering and my knees knocking.

A very real satisfaction for me has been my altering relationship to a young woman who happens to be my daughter. Sarah and I recently had a long conversation in which she expressed gratitude that, as a result of her experiences, she was moving from childhood into adulthood, into an acceptance of her womanhood, acquiring the ability to deal creatively with being alone. Until now, she said, she felt lonely and scared when she was not with people and did not have a radio or TV going.

It was a beautiful conversation and at the end of it, I was given the courage to ask for a gift from her. I asked if she could let me come down from the pedestal—the pedestal of parent, of father, and of omniscient guru. I asked if she could allow me to be a human being to her. I guessed that would mean disappointing her many times, but it would free me to be myself with her.

This was a big step for both her and me, but she agreed to move with me in that direction and to spend more time with me on the patio. Since then we have succeeded some and failed some. It's tempting for me to speak to her from above and it's tempting for her to let me do that, but I believe we are risking and growing.

I'm also trying to overcome my envy. It is very difficult for me to be magnanimous about someone else's talents, especially if they result in acclaim and status. I recall with some dismay lunch conversations with academic colleagues in which it was almost *de rigueur* to speak slightingly about the publications or achievements of people who were threatening to us. A favorite form of put-down was, "He's said all that before. Why does he need to say it again?" Or "He got all that from Gadfrey. He wrote his dissertation under Gadfrey and the book is just Gadfrey warmed over." Or "She's written a good book, but she seems rather pugnacious in her manner, doesn't she?"

I blush when I remember that. I think I tried manfully to become less envious, but the disease does not respond to simple willing. It needs stronger measures. I now see that the best medication for my envy is to meet on the patio the people I resent, and to see them as human beings who are my brothers and sisters in Christ. When I can see my competitors as persons, they become less threatening to me. When I can accept them and feel accepted by them because God has accepted us in Christ, I can begin to love them. And out of my love for them flows gratitude to God for the gifts they are using to his glory. Envy still lurks in the corners of the patio like a disconsolate toad, but it is no longer a monster which threatens to destroy.

In Chapter 4 we shall talk about life-style on the patio, a style encouraged by the Holy Spirit. On the patio the personhood, feelings, responses, and behavior of fellow Christians are seen as gifts of ministry to me and—sometimes to my surprise—my personhood, feelings, responses, and behavior are gifts of ministry to them. Absolute democracy in Christ exists on the patio, where caring and sharing are straight across, blessing both those who give and those who take.

GROUP DESIGN 3

On a piece of large newsprint or a chalkboard, draw the design of the two towers. This is essential if the study is to be understood. Provide ample time for questions, but avoid quibbling about details.

After the study has been presented and the towers are understood, groups of four or six can be formed to discuss the following questions:

1. On what floor of my tower am I most comfortable, especially when I am feeling anxious and insecure?

2. What is most inviting for me on the patio and what is most difficult?

3. If the patio is a symbol of the church *in relationship,* what spiritual gift (as distinct from talent) do I find there which is specifically mine to share?

Life-style
on the patio

We began our study by alluding to the time when the Spirit of God moved over the waters, over the emptiness and void of the uncreated universe. We considered the creativity of the Holy Spirit in us, the establishing of our personal identity and the releasing of our power. In Chapter 3 we talked about how the Holy Spirit brings us together in true relationships on the patio.

The twin towers we talked about have been given to us by God and there is nothing wrong with them. God has given us our talents, the capacity to develop these talents to acquire skills, the roles and tasks by which life goes on and out of which may come status and, in some instances, preeminence. But the urgent question for us if we are going to be creative people is, Where do we find our identity and our fulfillment? For me the place of identity and fulfillment is the patio, between the towers, where I am in relationship with God, myself, significant others, and the world.

If I allow the patio to be the arena of my identity, then I can move more comfortably up into the tower and use my talents and skills or do a task without getting isolated in it. I know where I am at home and I can return there.

The church as a patio

Churches develop institutions for ministry. They must be organizational to stay alive. To keep the organization intact they must discover and train talent, encourage the development of skills, support role identification, and provide payoffs of status and preeminence.

Churches and Christians are "in the world" and every effort to deny that has tended to prove the contrary. Strained and sometimes frenzied idealism intended to lift people above their humanity often ends in disillusionment. The followers of Benedict of Nursia end up as Chaucer's Monk and some of the friars of Francis emerge at the end of the Middle Ages as venal and lazy beggars, drones in the busy beehive of the world's work.

But to be *in* the world does not mean being *of* the world, that is, conforming to its patterns of isolation and competition. Perhaps churches would do well to be more concerned with the patio and less preoccupied with every other level in the towers. The church is called upon to model a community of caring and supportive relationships, to incarnate a life-style of honesty and love. No organizational imperatives, however urgent, should allow us to discount the *being* of the body of Christ.

I lived and worked for many years in a denomination which, like every other denomination in America that I know anything about, devotes enormous energy to keeping its organizational house in good repair. During all that time I did not know that my real function was not to develop institutions and programs, but to foster loving relationships. I was so preoccupied with my talent as leader, with my skill and training as educator, with my power as administrator of a college and seminary, with my related status and with other dignities I assumed that I thought very little about living on the patio and finding my personhood and relationships there.

In Colossians 3:8-17, we are given a list of undesirable as well as desirable responses for the Christian community. This passage is a model of a functional Christian life-style.

Paul tells the Christians in Colossae:

- To get rid of anger, passion, and hateful feelings
- Not to speak insults or obscenities or lies
- To be compassionate, kind, humble, gentle, and patient
- To be helpful and forgiving
- To love
- To accept the peace of Christ
- To celebrate

The heart of this teaching is the value of personhood in the new order of things which Christ has established. Not only are the paganisms of immorality, lust, evil passions, and greed to be killed off. The believers in Colossae are to look at one another in a new way, recognizing the worth of personhood and finding the meaning of life in relationships based on love (Col. 3:1-7).

Feelings on the patio

This new life-style is not to be equated with mere niceness or sweetness. The American tradition of being nice to people, from whatever motives, keeps relationships superficial, denies real conflict, and makes loving and caring impossible.

Hence the first step is to go to work on yourself and deal with feelings which are destructive to you and others. In Colossians 3:8, Paul lists these destructive feelings as sudden fury or rage, wrath or ongoing hostility, malice or hate, and eagerness to harm another.

We need to pause here to deal with a very complicated point. It sounds as if Paul sees these feelings as evils which must be dealt with through the operation of grace. But the destructiveness of rage, hostility, and malice lies not so much in the feeling as in how I act it out. Because of misunderstanding on this point, the church has encouraged sitting on negative feelings. As a result, angry people turn their anger into depression, sullenness, or endless nit-picking.

People living the patio life-style accept angry feelings but seek to deal with them honestly by encouraging verbal expression of them, by channeling the energies they generate into constructive effort, and above all by seeking to find their root cause.

The second set of things we need to deal with on the patio, Paul suggests, is the verbal expression of hostility. The Revised Standard Version translates the words in Col. 3:8b as "slander" and "foul talk;" Today's English Version renders the same words "insults" and "obscene talk." "Foul talk" and "obscene talk" suggest that Paul objected to the Colossians' language as violation of good taste. But the words mean "reviling" and "loud abuse," language used to "put down" and discount the other.

The pagan world seems to have been freer even than modern man in pouring verbal abuse on people. Reviling, obscenity, and blasphemy were indiscriminately mixed. We may be more decorous in our expressions, but we are just as capable of using language to undermine and destroy others.

Honesty

Paul adds a final injunction: "Do not lie to one another, because you have put off the old self with its habits, and have put on the new self" (v. 9).

Honesty is the keynote of the Christian life-style. Without honesty and all that accompanies it, no vice loses its power and no virtue is energized. Honesty is the climate of the patio. It encourages straight communication, prevents manipulation, and puts you and others into the daylight.

The climate on the patio is a bright and gentle air of compassion, kindness, humility, gentleness, patience, helpfulness, forgiveness, love, peace, and thanksgiving culminating in a celebration full of song and gospel. Because this is so attractive, I am constantly tempted to revert to my all-too-human pattern of untruthfulness to try to achieve it. On the patio, when I do not feel what I ought to feel or when I don't behave as I ought to behave, I am tempted to lie.

And so in that place created by the Spirit of truth, I create a cuckooland of phoniness and falsehood. I do not express what I feel. I am angry but I can't say it. I am tired but I can't admit it. I am bored but I smile pleasantly. I am scared but I breathe an air of cheery calm. I am sad but I don't let my tears flow. I am full of doubts, but I breathe only platitudes of faith.

That is how I deal with my feelings. That is also how I deal with my needs. Once I have begun to lie, it becomes an easy way to cope. I may not falsify my report of an incident and I may never cheat anyone out of a cent, but what I tell you about my needs is sheer soap bubbles. I am tempted to draw a veil of subtle falsehood over my relationships and never allow the real to surface.

I need only remind you of Jesus' forthrightness to indicate what honesty on the patio means. He seems never to have placated his opponents or to have denied his family, his followers, or his friends the gift of straight communication. He never tried to please anybody or to bind anyone's will. Even in his last hours he did not try to prevent Judas' betrayal or Peter's denial or the mad flight of his friends.

Vulnerability

In this I do not identify with Jesus, although I would like to. I have a very bad time with the truth about my feelings, my needs, my history, and my relationships, probably because I believe that if I tell you the truth about myself, you are not going to like me or you are going to get angry with me. And if you get angry with me, you are probably going to punish me, reject me, and ultimately abandon me.

I can't tell you about my needs because they will reveal me as a human being who has the same needs as you. I need to eat, be safe, belong, be loved, get strokes, and actualize myself. Our Lord was quite free about his needs. He could hunger, thirst, get weary, respond angrily, and

59

even question God's dealing with him. But I can't show you my clay feet.

I will also lie to you (in a subtle way) because I can't stand to hurt you. I need to protect and defend you from the pain of my truth. I don't have the courage to give you the gift of honest feelings because I don't believe that the truth will set us both free.

Honesty would make me vulnerable, so I shy away from it. But vulnerability is the bedrock of relationship. Without my vulnerability, you cannot tell me who you are. Without it I am a closed book to you and you to me.

This has been a very painful year for me because I have had to review the way I handle my feelings, my needs, my relationships. Circumstances, and no fresh-minted courage on my part, have forced me time after time this year to inventory my vulnerability, really to look at it. It has not been a reassuring experience.

After writing and speaking about an honest life-style for several years, I have to admit that I am tempted to temporize, rationalize, project, justify, and defend rather than to admit, confess, and repent. I continue concealing who I am.

I identify with Adam and Eve in the garden after their disobedience and their discovery that they were naked—intolerably naked. Their nakedness became a problem at the moment of their disobedience. The Scriptures seem to say that disobedience and openness are irreconcilable, that when we know that we have transgressed, we conceal, we look around for some means to make it look as if nothing has happened.

I am still a child of Adam and Eve. I fail and sin in

many ways, and when I do, I use my inventive powers to defend myself and to make me acceptable.

And I forget the patio. I forget there is a place where, in the company of the crucified and risen Lord and the members of his body, I can claim unconditional love. I forget "there is no condemnation now for those who live in union with Christ Jesus." I forget that if we confess our sins (that is, if we accept his gift of openness and vulnerability), "he will forgive us our sins and make us clean from all our wrongdoing." And I need to remember that. For life on the patio is intolerable if its presupposition is not that the people there "come as they are."

Love

Vulnerability, openness, and honesty are closely tied to another quality of equal value on the patio. Paul says, "Speak the truth in love." And love is an essential ingredient of life on the patio. Love in this context does not mean simply attraction or liking. Its meaning is revealed in God's love toward us. God's love is an act, a willing. The incarnation is God being with us on the patio. When we love another person, we can be with that person and identify with him or her without controlling. *Being with* means we enter into that person's life and share as much as we can of it. That is love. As Paul says, we are "happy with those who are happy, and weep with those who weep."

Control sometimes disguises itself as love. We think we love people when we do things for them, but if they could and should do those things for themselves, we may be controlling rather than loving. We sometimes do that

61

as parents. It's very tempting for Sally and me to try to control our children, even though they're all grown and married now. We try to love them by being with them without attempting to influence their decisions and without doing things for them which they ought to be doing for themselves. This kind of love doesn't rule out giving gifts, but it does require that we examine our gift-giving carefully to be sure that what may look like love and caring does not mask control.

Affirmation

Growing out of honesty and loving is the gift of affirmation. To affirm people is not to flatter them. Flattery may look like affirmation and it sounds good, until you realize it's exaggeration. Telling someone "You look like a picture" or "You look so young" when the opposite is true is not affirmation. It may be dehumanizing and depersonalizing. To affirm someone we recognize the worth of that person as a person, which is what Jesus did, and we recognize the real gifts that person has for ministry. On the patio "giving strokes" means we support and love people for what they are and for the gifts given them by the Holy Spirit.

In February 1968 I was speaking to a gathering of ministers in Galesburg, Illinois. Bruce Larson and Ralph Osborne, both active with Faith at Work, were to present a workshop to the conference the very next day and were hence in the congregation when I spoke. Afterwards, in the motel in Galesburg, we drank coffee together and talked. Both expressed appreciation for what I had said that evening. But I especially remember their attitude of acceptance and caring for me. People I knew and loved had tried to communicate the same feelings to me before, but I had not been able to receive them.

That night in Galesburg I breathed new air. It was almost like landing on a freshly created planet. I felt myself wanting to be with people like that and to be that sort of person. The previous summer I had learned for the first time what it was to accept myself. Now I wanted to be part of a fellowship of acceptance and affirmation.

Caring

If honesty leads to love on the patio and love issues out in affirmation, then it follows that affirmation results in caring. Henri Nouwen distinguishes between *caring* and *curing*. The original meaning of *care* is loud sorrow, an expression of loving identification with and investment in the grief of another. *Cure* comes from the Latin *cura* which is "care" or "concern," but which by usage has come to mean an intentional act of healing, remedying, or medicating.

Curing is fixing people up, straightening them out, and putting them back on the road. Caring is being with them. And there's a vast difference. If you come on to me as an expert or a guru or some kind of Mr. Fixit, you put me in an inferior position. In that situation I am the helped and you are the helper. That may be beneficial because we all have illnesses which need curing. But those who cure often remain uncared for and cannot admit their need of care. For years and years I was programmed to cure people. I went out of my way to try to fix them up and straighten them out. But I didn't then know how much care I needed myself.

Care is directed to our humanity, to our needs as people. We all have needs. Often the church has failed to see that. It has failed to see that it can be a community in which everyone is sensitive to the pain, as well as to the joy, of others.

Groups can benefit from a simple exercise—participants rubbing one another's necks. Caring for people involves touch. Jesus began with the little children; he placed his hands on them and blessed them. Caring for someone through touch is getting at their weariness and their weakness. Because we are all mortals, no matter how strong and how vigorous we may seem, we require that kind of caring. Such caring can be done many ways, and none of them is without risk. But we need caring by nonseductive touching in our religious community. Rubbing the neck of someone who is tired and tense may say to that person, "I'm with you. I also have a neck and shoulders that get tense and tired. I'm not here to fix you up! I am not a physical therapist. I just want to be with you and care for you. And I want to be cared for in turn."

Some time ago I was going to a weekend of services in a church on the East Coast. I was tired and sad and I had a bad cold. Before I began preaching Friday night I said to the gathered congregation, "I just want to tell you that I'm not in very good shape. I have a terrible cold and I'm tired and sad. I want to care for you but I also need to be cared for. Let's make this a weekend in which we care for one another." At the end of that weekend, several people came to me and said, "This is the

64

first time we have ever had an opportunity to care for the minister."

So many of us convey the image that we are above the need to be cared for. We are strong and we can be leaned on in all circumstances. And we can't let anyone down. Not the church. Not even God.

At a conference I attended participants were asked to fashion from clay something representing what we were feeling. Myron Maddon, my friend and coworker, made a little bird with the biggest mouth I've ever seen. He pried the mouth wide open until the bird seemed all mouth, and he said, "I'm just waiting to be fed." He was sad because he saw himself always giving out, always nourishing other people, and never having much chance to be fed himself. But the patio is refuge for everyone. It is a place where all of us can care and be cared for, nourish and be nourished.

Confrontation

And curiously enough the patio is also a place of confrontation, where honesty extends to dealing with conflict in the fellowship. Confrontation—telling others if their behavior or attitudes trouble you—seems not to belong to the church. How can confrontation be put together with blessing and affirmation and caring and loving?

Loving confrontation makes caring possible. Jesus was a fantastic confronter. So was Paul. He was always confronting somebody. He seemed to enjoy it a little too much. First he confronted the Christians. Then when he became a Christian, he still confronted the Christians. He wrote confrontive letters to the Corinthians and the Galatians. And he had a confrontive go with Peter in Antioch. But we can share our feelings in confrontation on the patio in a way that reinforces loving and caring.

The thought of confrontation scares me to death. I hate to be criticized. I see some people begging for feedback. I admire them. I don't beg for it. If somebody says to me, "I have something I need to tell you," my stomach starts churning, my mouth gets dry, my heart pounds, my blood pressure goes up dangerously high. Does anyone like to be confronted?

Still, I want to learn from those around me. It will be evidence of growth for me if I can see confrontation and feedback as acts of love. It is an act of love when people tell me how I'm coming through. Jesus says that his father is a gardener who prunes every branch that bears fruit so that it will bear more fruit. What a loving act such pruning is! We too can give and receive loving feedback and caring confrontation on the patio. We are pruned in order to bear more fruit.

Celebration

Also on the patio, praise God, is the party, the celebration. Celebration does not mean carrying banners around without a reason. Someone has said, "You can't really shout 'Hosanna' until there has been a victory." Celebration is a Hosanna for Christ's victory in us. To celebrate is to lift life up to God in praise and adoration.

Probably the most nonspontaneous activity left in the Western world is the Sunday morning church ritual. Innovative services organized in many churches truly express victory in Christ. But often the routine worship service is planned to the last detail. The program is locked into print, and spontaneity is banned. Sameness and repetition provide security, but that kind of service is hardly a spontaneous overflow of enthusiasm and joy because Christ is victorious in us. The church service, too, can take place on the patio, the gracious place where, through openness and vulnerability, loving affirming, caring, nourishing, confronting, and celebrating, we can be healed and made more whole.

The patio life-style serves to draw down for common use the talents, training, skills, and roles I have developed in my tower; it also gives my tower experiences meaning and hope. If I know I can live on the patio, if I find my home there, I can witness among those who, caught in the isolation, competition, and defensiveness of the towers, have concluded that life has nothing more to offer them.

GROUP DESIGN 4

A few minutes may be needed to clarify more specifically the primary qualities of the patio life-style:

- Honesty, vulnerability, openness, with minimal defenses and concealment

- Love

- Affirmation, acceptance, sensitivity to gifts

- Caring, nurturing

- Confrontation and feedback

- Celebration

Print these on newsprint or a blackboard. Break into groups of four or six to discuss these questions:

1. With what element in the patio life-style do I have serious difficulties? Do I know why?

2. What element in the life-style is relatively easy for me? Do I know why?

3. In what setting, if any, am I most comfortable with this life-style: at home, at work, in church, with my friends?

The wine
of new gladness

The title of this chapter is from Dostoevsky's *Brothers Karamazov*. Alyosha, the youngest of the Karamazovs, has gone to the monastery late in the evening to pray by the dead body of Father Zossima. As he kneels by the coffin and hears Father Paissy read the story of the miracle of Cana, he falls asleep and dreams.

In the dream, Father Zossima comes to him and says:

> We are rejoicing. . . . We are drinking the new wine, the wine of new, great gladness; do you see how many guests? Here are the bride and the bridegroom, here is the wise governor of the feast, he is tasting the new wine. . . . Begin your work, dear one, begin it, gentle one! . . . Do you see our Sun, do you see him?"

> "I am afraid. . . . I dare not look," whispered Alyosha.

> "Do not fear Him. He is terrible in His greatness, awful in His sublimity, but infinitely merciful. He has made Himself like us from love and rejoices with us. He is changing the water into wine that the gladness of the guests may not be cut short. He is expecting new guests. He is calling new ones unceas-

ingly forever and ever. . . . There they are bringing
new wine. Do you see they are bringing the vessels?"

Something glowed in Alyosha's heart. Something
filled it till it ached, tears of rapture rose from his
soul. . . . He stretched out his hands, uttered a cry
and woke up.

The phrase "the wine of the new gladness" filled my
soul with rapture long before I believed it could exist outside the dream of Alyosha. I present it, not only as an
enchanting vision of what might be, but as an actual gift
for all of us. I believe that the wine of the new gladness
is available to those of us who at this moment believe joy
has run out.

The very first miracle that Jesus performed (John 2:1-
11) was taking care of a host's embarrassment at a party.
This seems to me to demonstrate God's inscrutable wisdom, love, and playfulness. Even the amount of wine in
the miracle (some 540 quarts) shares in the divine
whimsy.

Dostoevsky writes appropriately about it, "Ah, that
miracle! Ah, that sweet miracle! It was not men's grief,
but their joy Christ visited. He worked his first miracle
to help men's gladness. . . . 'He who loves men, loves
their gladness, too!' "

Let us walk into the situation at Cana when Jesus and
his disciples arrived for the wedding. Apparently the
mother of Jesus was there earlier and was acquainted with
the situation. Like many of us, she seems to have enjoyed
bringing news, even bad news. "They are out of wine,"
she says.

Jesus' reply to her is curt, almost angry. "You must not
tell me what to do, woman. My time has not yet come."

Having refused to give up his power to Mary and being confident that his time has come, Jesus then performs the miracle of changing the water into wine.

When joy runs out

Let us try to identify with the situation. There are times when we also run out of wine. The freshness, the joy, and the meaning go out of our life. We find with young Hamlet that "the uses of this world" are "weary, stale, flat, and unprofitable."

In my own life, I felt that "staleness" and "flatness" 10 years ago. Some people important to me had died, among them John Kennedy, C.S. Lewis, and Sam Shoemaker. If I was to believe some theologians, God had died also. I was deeply involved with college and seminary young people, and I saw that for them also the joy was gone. The smell of grief was everywhere, especially on seminary campuses. I did some grieving for myself, for the truth is that I was dead, or rather, God was dead in me. I looked everywhere for meaning.

The need to fix

I identify with Mary and, in doing so, I understand what the church has done to the relationship between Mary and Jesus. The Gospels are quite clear on this point, but the church as well as Christian artists from the earliest Middle Ages to the present have tended to portray the Mary-Jesus relationship as an ideal mother-son bond—all harmony and no conflict. This means Mary remains in control of the relationship by being the helper, the carer, and fixer. Insofar as it is legitimate to see the church as an extension of Mary, it is possible to perceive the church and each of its "curers" in the role of controllers of Jesus. So long as we cannot admit to a deep personal need to be cared for by Jesus, we are going to be programming him. This blocks his freedom and creativity and prevents his hour from coming.

But if we can cut through the Mother's Day sentimentality with which we have surrounded our Lord, we'll perceive that in several incidents he tries to distance Mary. She is no doubt important to him, but, as with every other mother, the parental role diminishes as the child becomes an adult. Hence the curtness, the firmness, and even the edge of anger which we perceive in the text. Jesus says to Mary, in effect, "Mother, you have your time; I have mine. You have your thing to do; I have mine." The mood is remarkably close to that in the Temple incident when Jesus was 12. "Didn't you know that I had to be in my Father's house?"

At the wedding in Cana, Mary comes on as Mrs. Fixit. She knows who's going to take care of the situation. Jesus is. This is not intended as criticism of Mary. She loved her son, saw his gifts, and wanted him recognized as the prophet he was. But, like many of us, she felt that she had to help the process along a bit.

When Jesus comes, she says in effect, "Don't just stand there. Do something." Mary seems to be a curer, trying to fix things up while floating above the pain. But Jesus is a carer who, rather than just trying to bring the pain to an end, enters into the situation in a loving and supportive way.

In the face of a critical situation, the curers rush in to

stitch, paper-clip, tape things together. "If the process is too painful, stop the process!" So runs their counsel. This hysterical need to stop the pain is more with the curer than the victim. I need to bandage your wound, though it may need much more thorough care, to shut out the sight of it from *me*. I don't want to see it. Sometimes the bandage is a verse of Scripture or a pious cliche; sometimes it is a word of advice. But whatever its nature, my intent with it is to fix things up in order to make myself feel more comfortable with the situation.

I identify with Mary. I have been a fixer, a curer. There was a time when I was very sure about what I wanted to do and what I wanted Jesus to do. If people don't have any wine, make some. If people are sick, start a health program. If people are bored, entertain them. If people have problems, get them converted.

I did not then see that in all those actions on behalf of people, I did not enter into their lives or their pain. I did not weep for anyone. And I did not let anyone into my life. In other words, my curing kept me from caring and from being cared for myself. In my need to be needed and to be important to people, I rushed around analyzing, diagnosing, counseling them, but rarely identifying with them or admitting that I myself needed help.

Correcting Christ's work

An incident from the *Brothers Karamazov,* which seems to be pushing its way into this study again and again without being bidden, is a commentary on the tension between those of us who try to program Jesus and his free, sovereign spirit. In Ivan's poem, Jesus appears before the

Grand Inquisitor as a prisoner about to be burned at the stake for heresy. The Inquisitor says to Jesus:

> "Know that I fear Thee not. Know that I too have been in the wilderness. . . . I too prized the freedom with which Thou has blessed men, and I too was striving to stand among Thy elect, among the strong and powerful, thirsting to make up the number! But I awakened and would not serve madness. I turned back and joined the ranks of those who have corrected Thy work. I left the proud and went back to the humble for the happiness of the humble. What I say to Thee will come to pass and our dominion will be built up. I repeat, tomorrow Thou shalt see that obedient flock who at a sign from me will hasten to heap up the hot cinders about the pile on which I shall burn Thee for coming to hinder us. For if anyone has ever deserved our fires, it is Thou. Tomorrow I shall burn Thee. Dixi."

In my curer role, I have to confess to a need to correct Christ's work. For many years I yearned to see people converted and joining what I conceived as the thinning ranks of the church. But my understanding of conversion was complicated by my growing awareness of emotional ill health. At the time I assumed the presidency of a liberal arts college and theological seminary, I had a strong conviction that religious conversion must go hand in hand with emotional wholeness. I still believe that, but I don't go about achieving it in the same way.

As the head of an institution with limited financial resources, I pushed through a plan of providing psychological counseling for any one of our 1600 students who, in the opinion of professionals, needed it. And I approved a plan of compulsory testing which would flag those in the student body who seemed to require such help.

We secured the services of highly qualified professionals—a psychiatrist, a clinical psychologist, a pastoral counselor, and some psychiatric social workers. The center did a beautiful job of helping people and I remain grateful to my colleagues who gave themselves so unstintingly to the ministry of caring. But I am not at all sure that we accomplished any part of what I had visualized. People are strangely free and Jesus is strangely free. And I'm afraid my effort to construct a Christian republic on the campus of our college was tinged with the megalomania of the Grand Inquisitor.

Like Mary, I was aware that the joy had run out for many people, and I envisaged a need for more wine. It had not occurred to me, as it seems not to have occurred to Mary, that a *better* wine is possible if we wait for Jesus' time to come. In my anxiety to get the decanters of gladness filled, I was willing to manufacture a substitute which was a product of my own planning and my own brewing. And people remained thirsty.

I did the same thing in my own family. Sally and I have four children. When they were small, I wanted us to be the ideal Christian family. I wanted the children to be a carefully tended flock of domestic geese in the Christian goose pen, a flock of uniform though identifiable goslings. But those plans went awry. Our children are wild geese who sometimes fly in flock but who often fly magnificently alone and free.

A few weeks ago I spent some time with one of our sons on his sailboat. It was a varied weekend, swooping and dipping in blue, wind-blown waters and lying cozily becalmed in a harbor as the still night came on. Sunday morning we sat in the boat's cabin and talked about the past. He said to me, "You know, I got churched out when I was a child. It was too much." I didn't know what to say. And pain rose up in me, not so much the pain that he and I do not agree on the faith (although that is certainly there) as the pain of regret for what I had done to our children in trying to make them into what I wanted and needed. I could not wait for Jesus' time to come.

I am not saying we have no right to give our children the gift of faith or to witness to them about what the Lord means to us. That is our right and our responsibility. But we must also make sure that our expectations do not control them and that if they choose to turn their backs on the faith and the church, we see that, not as rejection of us, but as an assertion of their freedom to be the persons they are.

The new wine

So there it is. And here I am. I'm finally able to say, "People are thirsty and I cannot give them to drink." Then Jesus comes. His time comes. That is the gospel. Bach has a cantata called "God's Time Is Best." That's what Jesus said to Mary. "Wait till my time comes."

When Jesus did come to me and the wine began to flow again, it had almost nothing to do with what I had been doing or trying to do all those previous years. It was, as Dostoevsky says, "the wine of the *new* gladness." The host of the feast, or the master of ceremonies, tasted it and said, "This is better stuff than you have been serving all day." Jesus brought me and many other people the wine of the new gladness. That is a mystery which I cannot solve. I cannot tell you how it happens, I cannot set it up, I cannot control it. All I can do is bear witness to it.

I have lived in the church all my life. I have been an active participant in the life of the church. I have been a public figure 40 years. And I have sat through hundreds of committees and board meetings, filling up hundreds of pages of foolscap on suggestions for renewing the church—"How to renew the church in six easy lessons"— and I do not today have the faintest idea how you make wine out of water. I do not know how to renew the church or make it grow.

What I can do is perceive the miracle when it happens and bear witness to it. I can only put glasses on the table and ask you to wait. When his time comes, your glass will be filled. I politely suggest that you hold out your cup for the wine of the new gladness, presenting who you are to Jesus. He will come. And when he comes, the wine will flow and the party can begin.

During the Jesus movement in the early '70s, to my taste everything seemed wrong. Everything! The hammiest preachers seemed to be dishing out the most incredible stuff. First I said, "This is absolutely loony. It can't work." But then I saw pictures of young people being baptized in the waters of the Pacific by these "unqualified" preachers. The look in the faces of the converts was absolutely new, and I saw that the wine of the new gladness had begun to flow.

When the joy has run out, Jesus comes, and he gives us the new wine. Practically, that means he is in the business of making us whole. That's what he wants with us, and that is not sentimental. It's not, "When Jesus comes,

77

we can stop being adults." Rather, when Jesus comes, he puts us to work in the process of becoming whole. Paul says, "Keep on working, with fear and trembling, to complete your salvation, because God is always at work in you." That's what happens when Jesus comes. We start thinking more clearly. We get to work with our consciences, with our guilt feelings. We straighten out our decisions, our wills, our plans for our lives. We pay attention to our bodies. We acknowledge our feelings. We start working on our relationships. In his presence, because of the miracle, everything begins making sense again. And the joy starts flowing.

As I write these pages, I am in pain—not physical but emotional pain. I feel the trauma of retirement and self-employment. I am said, confused, and out of control. And that hurts.

But if I am in new pain, I am also in new joy because I am seeing things beginning in me. There are evidences in me that I am still growing, even though I am an aging man. And I would like to say with Father Zossima, "We are rejoicing. We are drinking the wine of new, great gladness. . . . Christ is changing the water into wine, that the gladness of the guests may not be cut short."

GROUP DESIGN 5

The leader may want to answer questions concerning terms from the Bible study, but should not encourage conceptualizing ("head-tripping"). This is a design best suited to groups of two. If the twos can leave the meeting room for a quieter spot, this may facilitate sharing. The questions are:

1. Where in your life, if anyplace, does joy seem to have run out? In your studies, your job, your marriage, your other relationships?

2. What are you inclined to do so the joy can return?

3. What would the "wine of the new gladness" look like to you?

4. How do you think it might be made available to you?

Hot
cross
buns

Chapter 5 of 1 Corinthians is not often read. Here
Paul talks about the old yeast or the old leaven. He comes
through shrill, and he has his parental toga on. He's
scared because the church he's helped bring into existence
is getting confused, and he writes them to say:

> Now, it is actually being said that there is sexual im-
> morality among you so terrible that not even the hea-
> then would be guilty of it. I am told that a man is
> living with his stepmother! How then can you be
> proud? On the contrary, you should be filled with
> sadness, and the man who has done such a thing
> should be put out of your group. As for me, even
> though I am far away from you in body, still I am
> there with you in spirit and in the Name of our Lord
> Jesus I have already passed judgment on the man who
> has done this terrible thing, as though I were there
> with you. As you meet together, and I meet with you
> in my spirit, by the power of the Lord Jesus present
> with us, you are to hand this man over to Satan for
> his body to be destroyed, so that his spirit may be
> saved on the Day of the Lord (vv. 1-5).

I do not understand Paul's judgment. But I do understand the feeling he is expressing. He is frightened. He
is concerned. So he comes on with a typical Pauline hyper-
bole. Then he continues:

It is not right for you to be proud! You know the saying, "A little bit of yeast makes the whole batch of dough rise.' You must take out this old yeast of sin so that you will be entirely pure. Then you will be like a new batch of dough without any yeast, as indeed I know you actually are. For our Passover feast is ready, now that Christ, our Passover lamb, has been sacrificed. Let us celebrate our feast, then, not with bread having the old yeast, the yeast of sin and wickedness, but with the bread that has no yeast, the bread of purity and truth.

At the time of the exodus, when the children of Israel moved from Egypt out into the wilderness and on to the promised land, they were instructed to make bread without yeast or leaven, so-called unleavened bread. God was saying to the children of Israel, "You have to say goodbye to Egypt, so take with you none of the old dough that has turned sour. Take only new bread which is unleavened. This is a new covenant and a new situation."

In dealing with the Corinthian church, Paul was confronting confused people. A serious situation had come up in the church, and the church could not handle it. I hear Paul saying to the Corinthians, "Is this the community of grace? A community of grace is not a laissez-faire society which lets anything happen. It is rather a community which deals responsibly with its people."

Old leaven

In Corinth, people were uncertain about how to go from the past to the present. The man who was committing the gross sin which upset Paul was a person who could not deal with his own past. He was living with his stepmother, a destructive and unhealthy way of relating to the past. This is an instance of a person within the fellowship who is not dealing creatively with his situation, and the church is doing nothing about it.

The situation in Corinth is not unlike what we find among people in the church or outside the church. We tend not to deal with the past. We bring it with us and it lies within, like fermenting dough or undigested food or unassimilated experience. Then it begins to poison our lives and we don't know what's happening.

Some of us carry with us into the present, dictims or moralistic messages given to us in the past, messages we never really accepted for ourselves. Certain rules were simply handed down to us and we live by them. When we were children, some of us were told, "Clean your plate!" And that old leaven remains. Even if we are overweight and shouldn't clean our plates, and our reason tells us we don't need to, the old leaven keeps working. So we sit down to the table and if we eat the food, the dictum comforts us and says, "Well, there are millions of starving people in China. You are a good boy or girl for finishing that."

"Grown men don't cry" is another dictum. And that's very comforting because often it seems easier to repress feelings than to deal with them, to let them come out. A man may cry only at his mother's funeral or while watching a sentimental TV film if it's dark in the room, hiding his face in his handkerchief.

"You've got to finish college." What a dictum that is today! Nobody can have stature in our culture without finishing college. Soon America will be crawling with unemployed Ph.D.s because the dictum says, "The more education you have, the better you are." We see these big ads, "Are you saving for your children's education?" It sounds almost like, "Are you looking out for the eternal welfare of your children?" So people kill themselves saving money as the colleges, out of dire necessity, raise their tuitions. Some miserable people become victims of that dictum. They cannot believe there is any option. But who says everybody has to have a college education? Who says a trade or a craft or a hobby is not a good way to make a living? The dictum says so. We live under these meaningless restrictions.

I met a man who was 50 years old. He grew up on a farm. He said, "I can't play. I've got to work." I said, "Why do you have to work?" He said, "I've always worked." On the farm you survive because you work, but now some unions are negotiating contracts which specify four-day workweeks. That's all people will need to work. Even so, there will be poor, unhappy people who get another job for the other three days. They will work a four-day week one place and a three-day week somewhere else because something inside says, "You can't play."

One day Sally and I were sitting in a restaurant in Columbia, Maryland, and some people came in who, because of their religion, were wearing very drab clothes. I said, "It's interesting, isn't it, that these people are doing this for the greater glory of God? They are honoring and serving God with their drabness. And this is the God who sows the meadows with flowers and spangles the skies with stars and gives us the mountains and the prairies and the seas—everything bursting with color. But they serve God, the God of color and the God of creative excitement, by being drab."

It's a dictum. Somebody said somewhere, "You shouldn't wear ornaments because. . . ." There's something in 1 Peter about women not "using outward aids to make themselves beautiful." In Peter's day decorated women were usually loose women, and Christians had a hard enough time living in the community without hanging that one on. And here is a whole denomination of modern people hitching their wagon to the star of drabness, dragging with them some old dictums they can't be freed from—old leaven that leavens the whole lump.

Controlling relationships

But "old leaven" is also the hangover of old controlling relationships. Most of us live too long with our internalized parents. People say, "I've got to go back and level with my parents." What they are really saying is that they want to level with the parents who are within them. My father is dead, but I have a lot of unfinished business with the father who still lives within me. The Corinthian man was living with his stepmother. Many people emotionally are living with their mothers or their fathers.

We can identify with the people in Corinth who hadn't thrown away the old leaven, and whose lives for that reason were blocked and corrupted. Our controlling relationships out of the past may cause us to need to be nice and to please.

This is where I am personally. Because of my early childhood, it is important for me to please. I am afraid that people close to me are going to walk away from me if I anger them. Hence I deal with their anger in one of several ways. I withdraw into myself. I behave evasively. Or I try to please.

During the past few months Sally and I have been facing problems in our marriage. This is painful to admit because we have been married a long time and we're supposed to have things worked out.

But a considerable part of the problem has been mine. I brought into the marriage some of the leaven from the past, and in my relationship to Sally I have been coming out of that. I have sometimes related to her as if she were my mother and in critical situations have responded to her by withdrawal, evasion, or pleasing. With her help, I am in the process of throwing away that old leaven and celebrating the feast with the unleavened bread of sincerity and truth.

Now you may ask, "What is wrong with pleasing people?" Well, there are two ways to please. We may please people as an expression of our love. If I love you, I may say, "I would really like to spend some time with you." That pleases you because it demonstrates my affection.

The other kind of pleasing comes not as a result of love but as bidding for love. I please because I am bargaining for approval. I'm trying to buy your love by doing what I think you want. That makes everything unreal and even phony. And that's "old leaven."

When I was 35 years old and I had finished my doctorate at the University of Chicago, I went back to my church and my denomination instead of staying at the university, which I had been invited to do. Why did I do that? Because in some ways the church was my mother and I had to please her. And I knew I would please her by going back and serving her, which I did for years and years.

I look back and ask, "Why didn't I have the freedom to say, 'Here are some of my options'?" But I had no options. With pleasing, there are no options. I had to please and I had to go back. I served faithfully, but I did not always serve gladly. God is marvelous. He turns even whale-blubber into perfume. And God can take a life that has been inhibited by old leaven and make something beautiful of it. I was blessed in what I did, but I probably did it for the wrong reasons, because of old leaven.

Old guilt

And there is old guilt. That too turns sour and becomes old leaven. James tells us that it can make us sick, and the psychologists bear that out. To get rid of old guilt, we must confess, not necessarily to the person wronged but to someone who in Christ's name can listen to our confession, pray for us, and communicate forgiveness and absolution. "Confess your sins to one another, and pray for one another, so that you will be healed" (James 5:16).

Paul tells the Corinthians, "Remember now, you can't just cover up stuff. You can't just not deal with it. You're backing off from this man, who's obviously confused." Paul has a way of dealing with him: "Hand him over to Satan!" That's a little rough for me. I don't know how to do that anyway. But Paul says, "Deal with it."

That's what we have to do with old leaven. Throw out the past, the repressive system of dictums that is killing you. Throw out unresolved guilt and binding relationships—whatever is controlling you. You're trying to make money. You're trying to please your mother or your father. You're trying to please your spouse or your pastor. These dictums come out of the past and they don't have your name written on them. They make you act in ways you haven't chosen. You can dump all that and turn to Christ. "God don't make no junk," but he can absorb ours. As the song says we can "take it to the Lord and leave it there."

I want to do that with all my old leaven—to leave it behind in Egypt, to let it lie. I believe God will take care of it. Heine is supposed to have said, "It's God's business to forgive sins." He said it cynically. I say it as a believer. And that's the gospel for me.

Easter bread

"Christ, our Passover lamb, has been sacrificed for us," Paul says. We don't have to endure the endless pain of dragging old leaven with us. We can eat the new bread of Easter. "Let us celebrate our feast, then, not with bread having the old yeast, the yeast of sin and wickedness, but with the bread that has no yeast—the bread of purity and truth."

If I were going to give 1 Corinthians 5 a name, I would call it Hot Cross Buns. "Hot cross buns, hot cross buns, two a penny, three a penny, hot cross buns." Hot cross buns are breads baked during Lent, very small and cheap.

Figuratively they are the bread of truth. They are the new persons Christ is forming in us. These small cakes of Paschal bread are evidence of Christ's work in us: a new willingness to share who we are, an awareness of new learning and new behavior, a claiming of our gifts, a willingness to ask for help from God and people, some joy or thankfulness for the power of his resurrection in us.

GROUP DESIGN 6

This design may require groups of two or three unless the level of trust and confidentiality in the larger group is such that groups of four, five, or six may work.

There are three questions:

1. What in my life can I identify as "old leaven" which robs me of power and which I would like to get rid of: dictums or injunctions out of my past which are irrelevant, binding relationships which need to be resolved, guilt that I have not dealt with?

2. Paul speaks of Christ as the "Passover lamb," sacrificed for us. He means that through Christ we can rid ourselves of the destructive part of our past and claim a new beginning. But we must claim it. The question is: How can I use my relationship to the people in this group (which I see as the body of Christ) to claim deliverance *now* from the past and a new beginning in grace and freedom?

3. What is a morsel of truth about me (the bread of sincerity and truth) that I would like to state and hence claim today? How can I describe the me I want to share with you?

The
walking
wounded

The story of Jacob's wrestling with God (Gen. 32:22-32) is a primitive and puzzling text and I do not dream of doing justice to it. Who, for example, is the dim figure who struggles with Jacob by Jabbok's ford? Is it a man or is it God? Or is it both? What is the connection between Jacob's night-long struggle and his reconciliation with Laban and Esau?

I do not have the answers to these and other questions, but the story, despite my puzzlement, continues to intrigue me.

Jacob is a complex person. He cheats his brother Esau of the latter's birthright and blessing. Later, as the employee and eventual son-in-law of Laban, the Aramean, Jacob responds to the cheating of Laban by conning him out of a substantial part of his flocks. When tension develops and Jacob decides to leave, he violates protocol by sneaking away with his family and his property without telling Laban. Jacob's wife, Rachel, adds insult to injury by stealing Laban's teraphim, or hearth gods, and then lying about it.

In his flight after some overtures to Esau, Jacob is informed that his brother is on his way to confront him.

Jacob is very frightened, for he knows that Esau has a score to settle with him. So he takes the steps we usually take when we confront a hostile person. He calls on the Lord to help him.

Jacob's prayer does not suggest the guilt he must feel, but desperate prayers are not subject to analysis. We can't cavil at a scream of pain. Jacob also arranges to try to appease Esau by giving him some presents. We are familiar with that tactic also.

In this context, Jacob has his experience with the dark stranger. The wrestling continues all night. Jacob will not give in and is finally injured in the thigh by his adversary.

When the day begins to break, the stranger tries to get out of Jacob's hold. But Jacob refuses to free him until he receives a blessing. The stranger not only blesses him but gives him a new name, *Israel,* meaning "contender with God." Jacob is convinced that he has seen God and calls the place *Peniel,* "I have seen God face to face, and yet my life is preserved." As the sun rises, Jacob limps away, crippled by the experience.

Life catches up

Despite the mystery of the text, let us try to walk into it and see what it says. I believe it says first of all that, for all our convulsive motions to avoid it, life catches up with us. Jacob must confront Esau. The chickens come home to roost. Ngaio Marsh, the detective story writer, reputedly said, "Send out telegrams to 100 people with the message, 'Flee at once; all is discovered' and 99 will head for the station or the airport."

A banker managed to accumulate a considerable amount

of money by embezzlement. He retired early and built a beautiful home on a hillside overlooking the city. One of his favorite spots was a patio facing the road which wound up the hill to his house. One day as he sat observing the road, he saw a police car move up the hill toward him. It turned into his driveway and out stepped two men who presented him with a warrant for his arrest. As he accepted the warrant, he said to them, "I've been waiting for you." The embezzler later told the press that from the moment of his retirement, he knew he would be arrested and brought to trial.

A second observation about the text is that we respond to the past with fear based on guilt. Jacob's fear of Esau is not only that the latter will kill him but that he has a right to do so.

My third observation is that when life catches up with us, our first impulse is to ask God to protect us from the consequences of our actions and to get us out of our difficulties. We may even do a little bargaining. If God will get us out of this jam, we shall serve him faithfully, never get involved like this again, make a generous contribution to the church or a favorite charity, and be good boys and girls forever.

The fourth thing I see is that, confronted with our fear and guilt, we try to atone, to set things right, to make it up to people. When he knows Esau is on the way, Jacob asks what price he will have to pay to "get off." He has conned both Esau and Laban. What is it going to cost him? This is a very common human response. Because guilt is so excruciatingly painful, we deal with both false and real guilt by asking for something to fix it.

I do not understand the mind of God, and I am not

saying he is unmindful of our prayers even when they are hysterical and manipulative. What I do see in the text, however, is that God reserves the right to determine how he is going to bless us.

Blessing and wrestling

And the blessing is related to the wrestling. I have heard this text used many times to support the need for importunate prayer. The examples of missionaries and evangelists are given: "Give me results or I die." The assumption seems to be that God is reluctant and needs to be persuaded to carry on his work. Hence the wrestling. I am not sure about the logic or the theology of that.

In the case of Jacob, the wrestling seems to have a different motive. The nameless stranger, who wrestles all night with Jacob and finally cripples him, serves to establish Jacob's identity and to give him a new name. Jacob in Hebrew means "supplanter," a suggestion of his tricky character. Israel, as indicated, means "contender with God."

This suggests that wrestling with God means the establishment of a deeper relationship with him, not with the intention of *doing* something for him but of *being* more fully what he intends, being more his person, which means being more Jacob, not less.

The close contact with the dark stranger leads to Jacob's crippling. He limps away. I suspect this is what an intimate grappling with the Most High means. God's divinity —his otherness—is confirmed by that experience. But so is my humanity. To wrestle with God means that my creatureliness blazes out. This is who I am. God remains nameless in that struggle. We don't know who he is. But we know better who we are.

Fear of blackmail

With whom do I identify in this shadowy tale? I do not like Jacob, for I have been tricked by sly people, but I have to confess kinship with that foxy man. Like Jacob, I live with fear of blackmail. Almost at birth I was implicated in the death of my mother. Since then I have tried to buy my way back into life by being good and responsible. But since I do not feel myself to be good or responsible, I have lived in fear of being discovered and punished. Yet I have also needed punishment, presumably so, I could set the record straight.

In all this, I have failed to accept who I am. I have not believed that by being myself I could escape the threats of the blackmailer. I knew myself to be moderately endowed with imagination and feeling, wit and humor, intelligence and sensibility. I say moderately, for I have no illusions about the depth or power of these endowments. But whatever their quality, I have never seen them as currency with which to confront my shadowy creditors.

In my tradition, and perhaps more important, in my pathology, I could not pay my way out of captivity by my artistic sensuousness (my delight in the beauty of color, sound, form, imagery.) The only valid medium of exchange available to me, I believed, was a mode of life opposed to the senses, namely the ascetic and spiritual. So I dedicated myself to religious vocations in which I could keep ahead of my creditors. In doing this, I sometimes went directly contrary to my identity and my gifts.

Most of my life I have been bored with the mechanics of devotion. I love the Bible because I think it's the most living and gutsy book I know, but I have never been able to chain myself to any routinized reading of it, chapter after chapter, verse after verse, and I don't believe that I have ever read it from cover to cover. That is because I have never been able to do anything day after day which was supposed to be good for me. Gymnastics, jogging, peddling my exercycle, systematic prayer, vitamin-enriched breakfast foods, meditative silences, and daily journal writing—all of it leaves me feeling bleak, as if a cloud has passed before the sun.

I am not saying that this is what most people feel or ought to feel. I hugely admire Puritan scholastics, Spanish mystics, Trappists, and Wesleyans who out of dedicated hours build intricate edifices of prayer and contemplation. But I am too mercurial, too volcanic perhaps, too impatient to follow in their train. And so I have lived with guilt and fear.

Self-acceptance

In 1944 I was in England with the United States Army, and I spent a night at Cambridge. It was a launching site for American bombers and was hence soggy with anxiety and grief. In the morning a friend and I went to King's Chapel for prayers. The incredible ceiling in flamboyant Gothic arched over us, but the stained glass windows were stored and had been supplanted by plywood and black tar paper. A few of us gathered in the choir and worshiped in the light of fluttering candles. The lection for the day was Psalm 107, and it was read in the old version, "They that go down to the sea in ships, that do business in great waters; these see the works of the Lord, and his wonders in the deep."

I can still recall the precise and elegant diction of the college chaplain who led us that morning. It reminded me that in this place prayers had been said daily since before the Armada. Devoted servants of Christ had met year after year to pray for people in difficult places just as we had met in the chill of that November dawn to pray for the men in the planes then thundering down the runways and out over the North Sea.

It was a moving experience and the images remain etched on the inner retina of my brain. But I have to confess that if I were a student at Cambridge or a tutor or a professor, I would probably not stumble out morning after morning for prayers. I am not a pious person. When I try to be, I become something other than I am: stiff, mechanical, artificially pleasing. This has been difficult to confront in myself and to accept. But I think that now, when my life is almost over, I am ready to do that.

Jacob was a contriver. In his encounter with Laban just before his wrestling with God, he is most defensive about his treatment of Laban. His father-in-law, he claims, has systematically short-changed him even though he, Jacob, has given the most unstinting service. But he does not mention his own trickery. There is no question that Laban is a con artist, but then so is Jacob.

I don't see that the confrontation with the dark stranger at the ford substantially changes Jacob's character. We look for that because we assume that the wrestling was a conversion or a second work of grace and that such a work makes people different. But if we study Jacob's meeting with Esau as it is recorded in Genesis 33, we have to conclude that Jacob's character has not been altered at all.

His reconciliation with Esau illustrates the point. Esau is blunt, warm, forgiving. Jacob seems oily and placating and a bit tricky. At the end of their conversation, Esau suggests that they travel together to Seir, with him in the van and Jacob following. But Jacob asks to travel more slowly on the grounds that his children are frail and his flocks unable to move fast. Esau agrees. The assumption seems to be that Jacob will come to Seir. However, as soon as Esau departs, Jacob and his party move on to Succoth and then to Shechem. The text does not tell us Esau's feelings, but they may be inferred.

I don't like to report this about Jacob because it is not an entirely happy ending. But it is reality. I believe the Holy Spirit is telling me that what was true of Jacob is true of me. I can and should change behavior patterns which are not helpful to me or others, but I am not sure I can change my identity, my essence, the *given* in me which is both my agony and my ecstasy.

But if Jacob is unchanged, what does his wrestling mean? I believe during the terrible night at the ford, for the first time in his life Jacob saw God face to face, that is, he saw things as they truly were in God's eyes. And he saw himself as he truly was. And he was not destroyed. He was crippled but he was not destroyed. He saw that he was Jacob and that would not change. He would still be the *supplanter,* the shrewd one, as we would say, an "operator," but he would also be *Israel,* "the contender with God." Because he was hurt in the thigh, he would go limping through life, "a walking wounded," but his injury would testify to the truth that he had faced himself, he had not tried to run away, he was no longer going to pay blackmail, and he had something real going with God. In the house of Laban, he had met his father-in-law's dishonesty with his own. He had lived perhaps more by his wits than by faith, and his fears of reprisals had made him a hunted thing. Then God stopped him in his tracks at the ford.

My own wrestling place

I am writing this from my own wrestling place. I am rounding out some days of solitary retreat at a frozen lake. It is mid-November and around the lake almost all the houses are dark and silent. Since I am a sociable person, this enforced aloneness has been painful. I have not been performing religious exercises, but I have been trying to get a hammerlock on the dark stranger who has met me here. Who is he? Is he the God of the patriarchs and the Father of the Lord Jesus or is he the mysterious other half of my own psyche, my unrecognized and unreconciled twin who, like Esau, keeps pursuing me?

I don't know, and it may not matter, since God reveals himself in many ways. But I am sure of several things. I know much more clearly who I am, not who I pretend I am or what others expect me to be. I am more ready than I have ever been to accept that *me,* even though that is risky and scary. I know in my guts that I can no longer confuse myself with God. I know that since I cannot bless myself, I must wrestle with him until he blesses me. (If, like Jacob, I have tried to steal the blessing, I'll have to have it authenticated.) I know I will have to go limping through life, honestly revealing my humanity and my quirky personhood and not pretend to be what I am not: consistent, smooth, adaptive, conforming, pleasing. All this is scary for me because I know I may make some people uncomfortable by being who I am, but that's the way it's going to have to be.

"I have seen God"

But my limping will also be publishing something else: "I have seen God face to face, but I am not destroyed." And that is the gospel for me. The gospel is that in Christ, God calls us into an honest, risky, painful, joyous, loving, and blessing intimacy with himself. Out of that intimacy does not come a race of standardized automatons or super-people, Christian heroes and heroines "without fear and without reproach." Out of it comes, rather, a regiment of "walking wounded": bloody, battered, weary, dirty, sometimes ashamed of the way they hobble and limp, sometimes fiercely glad that, though the night was long and hard, they managed to hang on.

I feel that I have lived a long time and am grizzled and graying, but I hope that when the dawn comes, it may be said of me as it was said of Jacob, "The sun rose upon him as he passed Penuel, limping because of his thigh."

GROUP DESIGN 7

Years ago, a psychology professor made a statement which has been very helpful to me: "God is able to use very imperfect tools." This design is to help us see that the biblical characters we are inclined to pedestal and make perfect are not super-people but very human like all of us. Since many Christians have been taught not only to reverence the Bible but to raise biblical characters to an especially exalted place, it may be helpful not so much to argue the point as to have the entire group suggest characters from the Bible who are very much like us, for example, Moses, David, Solomon, and the disciples of our Lord.

The groups may be fours or sixes. Sharing will center on the following questions:

1. What are my feelings when I see Jacob as a human being like myself?

2. How much of my present self do I see as the product of my own or other people's expectations of me and how much do I see as my authentic self?

3. What would "wrestling with God" look like to me and what would I expect from it?

4. How do I feel about being "walking wounded" for the rest of my life?

Small change, big change

The basis of this chapter is a well-known passage from Acts 3:

> One day Peter and John went to the Temple at three o'clock in the afternoon, the hour for prayers. There, at the "Beautiful Gate," as it was called, was a man who had been lame all his life. Every day he was carried to this gate to beg for money from the people who were going into the Temple. When he saw Peter and John going in, he begged them to give him something. They looked straight at him and Peter said, "Look at us." So he looked at them, expecting to get something from them. Peter said to him, "I have no money at all, but I will give you what I have: in the Name of Jesus Christ of Nazareth I order you to walk!" Then he took him by his right hand and helped him up. At once the man's feet and ankles became strong; he jumped up, stood on his feet, and started walking around. Then he went into the Temple with them, walking and jumping and praising God. The whole crowd saw him walking and praising God; and when they recognized him as the beggar who sat at the Temple's "Beautiful Gate," they were all filled with surprise and amazement at what had happened to him.

Peter and John went to the temple, but the action passes over to Peter, and he's the one who talks and the one who acts. He's the one who does everything. He's the leader of that little group. Poor John seems to be along just for the ride. And this is the same Peter who is in the Gospels and the same Peter who turns up in the Epistles. Everywhere you find the same Simon Peter always leading the procession and sticking his neck out and taking charge and being a manager.

Small change

I too have dedicated my life to the temple. I see the beggars with their hands out, expecting something, but not very much. And I see also that most of the people who gather at the Beautiful Gate of the temple expect something, but not very much. I am among the people who are needy and hoping that something is going to happen, but I don't normally expect very much either. I identify not with the apostles, but with the lame beggar.

I see people come to church for a Band-Aid or some mild medication for a particular need. Every week I get reprints of sermons from around the country. I keep asking: Is this sermon, which is carefully prepared and beautifully printed and distributed, being received as the word of life by the people who hear it or read it? Are they expecting great things from it? Are they expecting not small change, but big change?

I am reminded of a scene that used to be played out in the Army. In the morning on my way to the chapel, I used to go by a battalion medical dispensary. The dispensary was just an ordinary cantonment building. The walking wounded would sit on benches inside. These men were not really wounded, but they had a variety of ailments. Every morning some of the same people reported for sick call—those who didn't want to go to the rifle range or do close-order drill or hike 30 miles. They were at the Beautiful Gate, putting their hands out for a little APC, a routine pill for people who weren't very sick. Once the reluctant soldiers clutched those little pills in their hands, they could be sent back to the barracks or to some limited duty. They had then fulfilled their day's mission—to defend their country against the foe in the best way they knew how, which was to be as physically inactive as possible.

I've laughed some about that because that's the way I am. Maybe you are too. We have aching backs and sore throats and all kinds of reasons for not going anywhere. We just want the life process sustained. We ask society to pump something into us through a tube so we can make it through another day.

What these men wanted, of course, was to get out of the military. At least, that's what they thought they wanted. But I ran into a few of them after the war was over and they said, "Oh boy, I wish I could get back into the service. That was the life!" Out in the great, horrible world they hadn't found a bench where they could sit and wait for their APCs.

In the conventional cathedrals and churches of Europe, the chancels usually face east, toward the resurrection of Christ. The south gate of the transept is the Baptismal Gate, where life enters and where children are christened or baptized. At the north end of the transept, the door is called the lych gate, or corpse gate, because that leads into the cemetery. Through that gate the dead are carried out. You come into life through the south door, and you are carried out through the north door.

Are we content to just be brought in, sustained for a while, and then carried out? I see this mentality at work in myself and in other people. We are really afraid that the church is going to get alive and powerful. So we're like this beggar. I don't want to pun on this exactly. Yes, I guess I want to pun on it! The beggar asks for "small change," and doesn't really know about the big change, or if he knows about it, he doesn't really expect it. He is a man of small expectations.

"You bind your heart with triple brass," says Robert Louis Stevenson. That means that you settle in, gut it out, and don't expect too much. I may reason, "If I don't expect too much, I will not be disappointed." Have you heard that philosophy? If I reach my hand out I may get a nickel or, on a good day, maybe a quarter. That is what I grow to expect from the wisdom and the power and the love of God.

Big change

We need to remind ourselves that the gospel is at work in the church. Here is really good news!

We are sometimes careful to keep that truth caged. We make the Bible as ornate as possible. Once I was in an Army chapel where somebody had donated an elaborate brass pulpit made like an eagle with its wings outspread. On its back is an enormous folio Bible, which must have cost $100 or more to print. And the Bible is flying at people on the back of the eagle. I'm usually expressive when I preach. Sometimes I used to swing my hand around the front of the pulpit and end up with my finger in the eagle's mouth. What this said to me is that the Bible on the eagle's back is no one's good news. It's beautiful but it's meaningless, whereas the Bible as God's living Word is hot off the press. It's good news.

I like the title of the Bible: Good News for Modern Man. And I like a Bible with big type. I carry one around, and people say, "Do you have trouble with your eyes?" My eyes are good, but I like big type because it makes the Bible leap out at me, like a headline. It's good news —the good news that healing and wholeness are possible. We can be healed. We can be changed.

When this poor beggar puts out his hand to Peter and says, "May I have a little something? Some little something? Please?" Peter says, "I haven't got something to give you. I have everything to give you. Is that what you want?" What do we want? What do we expect? Do we really want the good news? Because then first of all, we have to reckon with Peter, who's very peremptory. "Look at us," he says to the beggar. And this man, who has been looking at his feet for a long time, lifts his eyes and looks into the eyes of the apostle. Then Peter says, "I *order* you to walk, in the name of Jesus." And Peter goes over and grabs the beggar by the hand.

Source of change

That shows us what we need to do when we want to change. *We need to focus in on where the change is coming from.* I see it coming from Jesus and through his people, often through small groups. But we don't just get people together in groups. With the Holy Spirit, we help create the body of Christ. Christ is ministering through everybody in the group. It is important to focus in on that, to believe that when you go into a group, Christ is there and *if you want help, you can get it.*

That's scary. It's so much easier to give help. To give help leaves us in control. But to accept help and to believe that this is Christ's body and that his Spirit is present takes away my control.

The next thing I need to do is *respond to help when it comes,* accept it, like the beggar. Peter reached his hand out and helped the beggar up. Then the beggar's "feet and ankles became strong; he jumped up, stood on his feet, and started walking around." This gives us the order of healing: we reach out, we get help, and then we take charge of ourselves.

This is important for me, for I am inclined to be dependent. I would like to have other people do for me some things I need to do for myself. After the process of being healed—and this has to happen again and again—instead of taking charge of myself, I would like to give that responsibility to someone else. But, like the beggar, I need to stand on my own feet.

Find the fellowship

The man went into the temple with Peter and John. This says to me: *find the fellowship, stick close to the fellowship,* because even though we are in charge, we need to ask for help. When Jesus is present among us, we find the fellowship, look into people's eyes, laugh with them, cry with them, hear them, share ourselves, care and are cared for.

This ultimately issues out in celebration. You cannot experience the body of Christ without beginning to feel the bubbles of gladness move up from the deepest wellsprings of your being. You can't help but celebrate the moment. The beggar did. "He went into the temple with them, walking and jumping and praising God."

We don't see much of that around conventional churches, and if we did we would probably call for an ambulance. But we need not show our joy physically. If you are staid and stable and celebration scares you, you don't have to go jumping and praising God outside. But if the big change happens, we'll be celebrating inside.

We can be like the little boy who was just beginning to discover he was a person and he had some rights. He was standing up in his high chair. His father said, "Sit down!" Still he stood. The father made a few menacing gestures (six feet two against two feet six) so the boy sat down. Then the father went out of the room, and the little boy grabbed the arms of his high chair and said, "But inside I'm standing up!" Inside you can leap and praise God.

Implication of miracle

The beggar probably had a fairly good life, because other people were in charge of it for him. But then suddenly he has whole feet. He puts one foot out of bed and it's sound and whole, and he puts the other foot out and that's whole too, and he says, "Oh, dear God, now I've got two legs that I've got to use!" Now he can walk.

Now he can't beg. Now he must work. It's a terrible situation to be in! He crawls out of bed testing his feet. He may half hope he's going to collapse and have to be taken over to the Beautiful Gate in an ambulance.

After healing, there has to be change. That's scary. Suddenly you have to stop being dependent. You have to be your own person. You have to go to work. That is what Paul means when he says, "Work out your salvation. And keep working at it, because grace is flowing into you." That doesn't mean you can lie down and put your hand out. It means you keep struggling to relate to people, to keep channels open, to stay honest and straight, to keep from manipulating and exploiting people. I believe Jesus went with that beggar, so in the lonely room where he awakened in the morning, he could turn to Jesus and say, "Hey, I'm not sure I want to be well."

It is risky and scary to be healed. Sometimes it's easier to be an object of pity rather than a responsible adult. We have to say to Jesus, "I'm not sure I'm going to be an adult all the time. I want you to know that. And I'm going to fail. But I want to go that way.

We will be vulnerable and we will hurt, but we can do it. We can learn to be responsible adults. We have to face our inner problems and ask Jesus to help. It's hard to ask him, "Where do you see me still unwhole? Where do you see me in need of healing? Where do you see me getting back into the child who just wants to please and be good to earn approval?"

It's hard to ask Jesus, because I know he'll say to me, "I want to make you whole, if you want to be whole."

And that leaves it up to me.

GROUP DESIGN 8

Plan time for a celebration at the close of the session. After input from the leader for the entire group, divide into fours or sixes and discuss these questions:

1. Where in my life have I been satisfied to ask for "small change"—in my relationships, the use of my gifts, physical and emotional health?

2. Where in my life am I ready to ask for a miracle of change or healing?

3. What would be the implications of that healing in my life and how would I handle them?

When the small groups have discussed the questions, the entire group may want to assemble for singing and for reporting on the questions. This should be brief, specific, and practical. Encourage participants to report significant learning or insights, decisions to change behavior, or resolutions to deal with a significant relationship.

The evening may close with some spirited singing involving body or hand movement ("I Am the Church, You Are the Church," "Lord of the Dance," or children's songs such as "His Banner Over Me Is Love" and "This Little Light of Mine"). A simple bread-breaking or agape with the passing of the peace of Christ may be a fitting conclusion.

Guidelines for ten relational Bible studies

THE LAUGHTER OF FAITH AND OF UNFAITH

Scriptural Content:
Genesis 18:1-15; 21:6-8; Hebrews 11:11-12

The heart of this text is the word of the heavenly messenger, "Is anything too hard [wonderful] for the Lord?"

The context is the Lord's visit to Abraham and Sarah. The patriarch is living like a Bedouin sheik in his tent at Mamre when three men appear to him. Like a good host, Abraham arranges for a meal of bread, roast veal, milk, and cheese. This seems an ordinary occasion on an ordinary day. Days come and go, people come and go.

But this is far from a commonplace occurrence. Heaven nudges earth. The guest is not routine; he is the Lord. All of a sudden the future bursts open to Abraham like a gigantic volcanic eruption. Nothing seems impossible.

Reactions to the revelation are interesting. Sarah, with the practicality of a wife born to a dreamer who associates with dreamers, laughs. A child? She knows better. Her laughter is an understandable snort of unbelief.

Abraham says nothing. He accepts. He is getting used to the astonishing God. At least he is getting used to being astonished.

Within the appropriate time Sarah gives birth to Isaac and says, "God has made laughter for me; every one who hears will laugh over me." This is the gentle laughter of faith and of delight. Now Sarah truly believes. Nothing is too wonderful for the Lord.

Application

Modern technology's emphasis on cautious inferences, control, and predictability has helped to make the laughter of unfaith even more general than in the day of Abraham. We hesitate to believe because we fear the ridicule of common sense.

But a revolution is on the way. Young people in the counterculture has refused to be bound to the wheel of rationality and social control. They are asserting their freedom in many ways, some of them foolish and destructive but some wise, creative, and liberating. These people believe that out of a culture growing cold and old and cynical, a culture of promise may be born. And they are acting on their faith.

The word in Hebrews 11:12 has been helpful to me: "Therefore from one man, and him as good as dead, were born descendants as many as the stars of heaven." Being near formal retirement age, I was yielding to the expectation of my years when the Lord spoke to me and said, "Is anything to hard [wonderful] for the Lord?" That word and the faith it inspired has given me new motivation, a new program, and new delight.

Questions

1. How do I find myself generally responding to God's promises to me: with the laughter of faith or of unfaith?

2. What particular miracle would I like to see happen in my life? If it happened, what would be my likely response?

PUTTING AN END TO GRIEF

Scriptural Content: Samuel 12:15-23

This passage describes the sickness and death of the child born of the union of David and Bathsheba. The union resulted from David's destructive action, ending in the death of Bathsheba's husband, Uriah, and in the wrecking of a marriage and a family. God had spoken through Nathan the prophet, rebuking David for his sin.

But a child had been born of the new marriage and David was no doubt hoping that something new would emerge from the old mess. Then the child became sick.

David reacts with great anxiety. He prays to God, he fasts, he lies prostrate on the ground. But despite this sincere act of repentance on David's part, the child dies.

David's elders and servants hesitate to break the news, fearing that grief will push David closer to the brink of madness or even suicide. But he surprises them. He gets up, bathes, changes his clothes, worships God, and then sits down to eat. In other words, he resumes life. During his fasting and weeping, he lived between grief and hope. Now that he knows the baby is dead and cannot be brought back, he accepts reality. And under that reality, like solid bedrock, is the faith that in this as in all matters relating to David, God has acted.

Application

There is "a time to weep, and a time to laugh," says the Preacher (Eccles. 3:4). In other words, there is a time to grieve and a time to stop grieving. The steps of grief (denial, anger, bargaining, depression) have become familiar through the work of Elizabeth Kubler-Ross. As she indicates, there is a time for *acceptance*.

This is so whether we grieve for the loss of a person in death or for loss of occupation, relationship, place of leadership, or way of life. Or even for the loss of a possession significant to us. We need to give ourselves to the grief process and feel our emotions rather than sit on them, but the time comes to resume living: to stand on our feet, bathe, worship God, eat, and walk the streets of our town.

Questions

1. In what area of my life may I need to grieve for a loss by allowing myself to feel the emotions associated with it?

2. Where may I now need to accept a loss by taking decisive action as David did?

RANDOM AFFLICTION

Scriptural Content: Job 1:6-22; 2:1-10

Job has been a pious man, blessed by God in his family
and his possessions. Then disaster strikes. He loses everything. As background for this catastrophe, the Book of
Job gives us a scene in heaven in which Satan taunts God.
Job, says the Lord of Misrule, is righteous because it is
profitable to him. Take the profits away and Job will be
no better than other men. God gives Satan the right to
harass Job and eventually to take away everything from
him but his life.

Job's wife encourages him to curse God and die, and
his friends tell him that he is suffering because he has
failed God. But even though Job questions what God is
doing and even gets angry with him, he will neither curse
him nor admit there is any real equation between his actions and the misery he undergoes. The book ends in Job's
admission that God is beyond his understanding and that
he (Job) has been presumptuous to speak about the
mystery of God. Then God restores Job's fortunes.

Application

When misfortune befalls us—an accident, the serious
illness or death of a loved one, the loss of fortune—we
are tempted to relate effect to cause. When I was a young
pastor, one of my older church members was struck by a

114

car and seriously injured. In his half-conscious state, he kept repeating, "There's nothing I have done."

Sometimes we have a hand in what happens to us. If we abuse our bodies, they will respond with illness and breakdown. If we behave destructively toward ourselves and others, we may assume unhappy consequences.

But in other situations it isn't very helpful to blame anyone—God, other people, or ourselves. The tragedy is too random to be accounted for. While we continue to believe God is sovereign of his universe, the tragedy may well look like a jape of Satan, a cruel trick to rattle us and unsettle our faith.

In such a situation we do well to be honest about our feelings of anger, fear, and frustration, as Job was, but to keep on trusting God while our teeth chatter. It is true that God gives and God takes away; it is also true that ultimately he reveals himself to us.

Questions

1. What unhappiness in my life can I see as directly caused by a trait or action for which I must assume responsibility? How do I respond to that—by blaming something or someone else or by dealing with it?

2. What unfortunate situation in my life seems generally unconnected with who I am or what I have done? How do I respond to that—by self-pity, putting myself down, "cursing God," or trusting him in the midst of my pain?

BLESS YOU

Scriptural Content: Psalm 103

Psalm 103, a favorite for thousands of years among Jews and Christians, is a song of praise to God, his character, and his actions on our behalf. It is a panoramic painting in which God's deep love, broad sympathies, and generous caring are celebrated. The psalmist praises God's healing and caring, his concern for fairness, his openness about his future plans for us, his magnanimity and generosity—and, conversely, his lack of petulance and vindictiveness, his spacious love, his compassion toward human beings because of their dependency and mortality, the permanence of his love. The psalmist concludes by calling on all of creation to join him in delighting in God.

Application

Psalm 103 is a beautiful song. I would like to invite you to do a difficult thing with it: apply the song to yourself. Although the psalm deals primarily with our relationship to God, we can ask how much of God's life is reflected in our relationship to ourselves. Let us ask ourselves the following questions:

1. Am I concerned about caring for myself and being made whole?

2. Am I fair to myself as a total person, that is, do I try to identify my needs and to meet them?

3. Am I honest about myself? Do I try to understand who I am?

4. Am I magnanimous and generous toward myself, or do I punish, berate, nag, and overload myself?

5. Am I compassionate about my frailness and my mortality, giving myself the freedom to be who I am and being ready to delight in me?

These questions may seem initially arrogant or immodest, but keep in mind the good news that because God accepts you in Christ, you have the freedom to care for yourself and accept God's graces rather than to criticize and punish yourself for who you are.

Questions

1. In what part of my life am I less generous than God is toward me?

2. What needs in myself do I have difficulty identifying?

3. What particular behavior or trait in me gives me delight?

4. If the members of the group proceeded to praise God for my person and my gifts, how would I respond?

CLOSENESS AS RISK

Scriptural Content: Mark 2:15-17; 7:1-23

These two episodes from the ministry of Jesus deal with how the religious leaders of his day saw his behavior. Jesus ate with tax collectors and outcasts (publicans and sinners), and his disciples and he ate with hands that had not been ceremonially washed.

The critics of Jesus saw righteousness as separation. The law-abiding person did not associate with law-breakers; he separated himself from them. The law-abiding person did not eat ceremonially unclean foods; he separated himself from them. He tried to remain undefiled by people or things that might contaminate him. Hence he emphasized isolation, apartness, and control.

Jesus saw righteousness not as separation and control but as closeness and involvement, which would issue out in healing. In the incarnation, God was tenting among human beings, not because they were good but because God loved them. And love always brings with it risks of infection and contamination. Control reduces such risks; contact increases them.

In his ministry, Jesus sought out needy people and brought them healing. He came in contact with sick people and identified with them. He came in contact with sinful people and identified with them. In a daring phrase, Paul tells us that Jesus "became sin" for us. But at no point did Jesus accept sickness as health or sin as righteousness. Inwardly he remained healthy and whole. He lived in a close relationship to God. No external contact could make his heart unclean.

Application

There are two life-styles presented in this text: the style of control and the style of contact. To maintain control, we need to separate and isolate ourselves from people, particularly those who are risky. But if we separate ourselves from people, the chances are good that we shall also isolate ourselves from God.

Contact is much less comfortable, and in making contact with people we risk making mistakes and even failing. Hence we need to maintain an open and healing relationship with our Lord and an honest awareness of ourselves. But we cannot wait until we are perfect to witness and serve. We must live in the confidence that he accepts us as we are and will bless us in the midst of our brokenness.

Questions

1. In what area of my life do I find myself trying to control people and circumstances because contact and intimacy are too risky?

2. How have I benefitted from risking closeness?

3. When has risking closeness caused me pain? Why?

LIFE DOESN'T STAND STILL

Scriptural Content: Acts 10:9-20

This is a story from the dawning hours of Christian mission. Cornelius, a Roman captain in Caesarea, who may be described as a seeker, is given a vision in which he is urged to invite Simon Peter to come to him. In response, Cornelius sends three people to Joppa to give the invitation to the apostle. Peter is staying in the house of some believers at Joppa.

While the messengers from Cornelius are on their way, Peter goes to the housetop to pray. There he has a vision of ceremonially unclean animals which he is told to kill and to eat. Peter responds that he has never done this, but the voice of God responds by saying in effect, "You'll have to change."

As a result of the vision, Peter begins to think deeply about the meaning of faith, and ponders what the vision could mean particularly in his own life. But while he is thinking, life does not stand still. The Spirit says to him, "Listen, Peter, there are some men looking for you, so get down from the housetop and go with them, in the confidence that I have sent them to you."

Peter obeys, follows the men to the house of Cornelius,

and is given an opportunity to witness to the gospel and to bring several people in the household to faith.

Application

It is striking how events crowd in on one another. In verse 19 we read, "Peter was still trying to understand what the vision meant, when the Spirit said, 'Listen! Three men are here looking for you. So get yourself ready and go down.' " This suggests that when the pace of God's action in history quickens, we are sometimes not given the luxury of the time to hesitate, deliberate, and study the meaning of our actions. It would be simpler if we were given the opportunity to identify causes and to look into the implications of events. There is comfort in studying fossil remains and even in appointing a committee to look more deeply into the practical consequences of our actions. But life does not stand still for us. In the midst of our thinking, life knocks at our door, and we are called to action. Even though the arrival of messengers from Cornelius implied a radical change in Peter's orientation toward the Gentile world, the Spirit gave him little opportunity to think about it.

This does not mean that careful thought and planning are always out of order. There is a time for deliberation and meditation. There is a time for interpreting the past and analyzing the present. After Saul's conversion, we are told that he spent considerable time in Arabia. No one knows what he did during that time. He probably studied the relationship of the Old Testament to the new faith he had embraced. But in God's economy thinking cannot be a substitute for action.

Questions

1. Where in my life does God seem to be urging me to a new attitude or behavior or relationship?

2. In the face of such a change, how do I find myself responding—hesitation, deliberation, postponement?

3. In what way does the Spirit of the Lord help me to decide and to act in obedience to God's will?

YOU CAN'T GO HOME AGAIN

Scriptural Content: Acts 21:37-40; 22:1-23; 23:11

The background of this particular incident is Paul's conversion and his witnessing for many years in the Gentile world to the power of the gospel. Now in closing out his ministry in Asia Minor and in the Greek world, he returns to Jerusalem, probably hoping he can continue his missionary work even farther west in Italy and Spain. In Jerusalem, following the urging of an old desire, he tries to share his experience and his witness with his countrymen, perhaps even with some of his old friends. He appears before the people with the apparent assumption that if he can speak persuasively about his encounter with Jesus, he may persuade them to embrace the faith which has changed his life.

But the effects of his witness are disastrous. What he says about a ministry to the Gentiles clashes with the view of his countrymen about religious faith. They see Paul as a threat to that faith as well as to them. The result is that some want to kill him. He succeeds in doing little more than creating an uproar. But despite the seeming fiasco of his experience, Christ comes to him in a vision and says, in effect, "Cheer up, Paul. You are really OK. I want you to go on to Rome."

123

Application

Good news is not always seen as *Good News* by the people we try to share it with. The truth of our witness does not guarantee its acceptance. Hence we may assume that sooner or later our life-style and our witness are going to be rejected. In that situation we need to keep some things in mind:

a) We need to understand our hearers when we try to share our faith with them. We need to be sensitive to the route by which they have come to the present moment, and not assume that changing a way of life is easy for the people to whom we witness.

b) We need to avoid being grandiose, assuming that our feelings and opinions and experiences deserve some kind of ultimate priority. A spirit of meekness and vulnerability will prevent our being unduly judgmental toward people who will not accept who we are and what we represent.

c) We must try to avoid adjusting our mood or even our faith and witness to our successes, believing that the truth we communicate is not dependent for its validity on the speed with which it is accepted.

d) We need to distinguish between our convictions and the way in which we communicate them. We may not need to change the content of our faith, but we may need to look at the way in which we share that faith with other people. In its evangelistic and missionary activity, the church has sometimes been incredibly arrogant. Instead of offering the gift of good news to people, we have laid the gospel on them as a demand and as a judgment.

e) We need to believe that it is not our task to change people or to make them over, but only to witness to God's work in us.

f) We need to understand that God has witnesses to his truth other than ourselves.

g) We need to leave the ultimate responsibility for success and growth and increase of his kingdom to God.

Questions

1. What has been my experience in trying to be more "open" and "relational" with family, friends, associates?

2. What do I see as reasons for the way people respond negatively or positively to me and my witness? What proportion of responsibility do I assume and how much do I attribute to them?

3. What does the comfort of Christ (Acts 23:11) mean in this situation?

THE SHAPE OF THINGS TO COME

Scriptural Content: Hebrews 11:1-3

We believe that God has made his word (his redemptive purpose with us) clear and graspable by coming to us in Jesus. "The word became a human being and lived among us. We saw his glory, full of grace and truth."

But the incarnation does more than reveal who God is and the meaning of what he has done. It is also the assurance of things we hope for, evidence of things we don't yet see. We see the shape of things to come in relationships. In our life together as members of Christ's body, we can have a foretaste of the coming glory.

Application

If this is so, we need not accept as normal and inevitable a personal life that finds contacts with God and people boring; family life that is merely routine and lacks warm, personal interaction; church life that is formal, external, organizational and lacks relational and personal warmth or is devoid of the joy of victory and celebration; a job that is only humdrum, carried out with an eye on the clock and the calendar.

This is not to say that much of life, work, and relationships is not rote. Learning multiplication, Greek verbs, or anatomy; practicing a musical instrument; reading proof; dusting furniture; weeding a garden; changing diapers; putting the same six bolts into 10,000 cars; making tents; being a bank teller, waitress, nurse, composition teacher—some of this is bound to be drudgery.

But much of life can be a foretaste of the glory which will be revealed. The key is inviting the Holy Spirit as the creator spirit into our lives, tasks, and relationships.

But inviting the Spirit means accepting the risk and pain of growth. This is where I block. I am afraid of change and so I barricade my life against the Spirit by trying to keep everything as it is. I welcome conformity, routine, tradition, sameness, boredom, if it will save me from putting out to sea.

But trying to keep things as they are and shutting out the Spirit erodes my faith, makes the future lifeless, and dulls the glory of heaven.

Questions

1. What specific thing in my present relationships (home, church, work) excites me and makes me hopeful for the future?

2. In what area of my life am I tempted to think that "as things have been they remain," that no change is possible?

3. To what creative change in my life would I be willing to invite the Spirit?